THE EVERY-DAY PHILOSOPHER.

THE

EVERY-DAY PHILOSOPHER

IN

TOWN AND COUNTRY.

BY THE AUTHOR OF
THE RECREATIONS OF A COUNTRY PARSON.

BOSTON:
TICKNOR AND FIELDS,
1865.

University Press:
Welch, Bigelow, and Company,
Cambridge.

CONTENTS.

CHAPTER IX.

CHAPTER X.

CHAPTER XI.

CHAPTER I.

TO WORK AGAIN.

IF you had slept last night in any one of the row of houses which forms the north side of a certain street in a certain city, you would almost certainly have been wakened up a little before six o'clock this morning by a most dreadful squall, which was the culmination of a stormy night. It was quite dark. The rain was driven in bitter plashes against the windows. The windows rattled, the doors creaked, the very walls seemed to tremble, and there was a dismal howling in the chimneys. For though the street I have mentioned has the city all round it, yet the ground on which it is built slopes so much, that the houses catch the unbroken force of the wind from the not distant sea. And from the upper windows, if you look to the north, beyond the gleam of a frith six miles in breadth, you may discern a range of hills, not far enough distant to seem blue.

It was a time in which to remember those who are at sea; and to be thankful that you were safe on shore.

But there is a further association with such a time, which would probably be present to the mind of many who in former days studied at a certain ancient University which the writer will never cease to hold in affectionate remembrance. For this morning was one of the latest mornings of October; and on the self-same morning in time, and on just such a morning for pleasantness, has many a student risen at six from his bed, that he might be present in the lecture-room, a mile and a half away, at half-past seven. On the previous day, he had gone at a comfortable forenoon hour to the Common Hall of the University, and assisted at the ceremony of opening the session. The ceremony was a simple one. Several hundreds of students, arrayed in gowns of flaming scarlet, assembled in that plain Hall; and heard the Principal give a short address on academic dignity and duty. And if the student were one who had studied at the University in former sessions, he would be cheered up somewhat in the prospect of resuming his studies by the sight of some familiar and kindly faces. But that ceremony in the early forenoon was but the gentle introduction to college-work; here is its stern reality. I am well aware that human beings in this world have oftentimes very dark and repulsive prospects to face, on rising from their beds in the morning; and I could think of things so grave as awaiting worthier men, that they make me almost ashamed to chronicle lesser trials. Yet I can say, from sorrowful experience, that duty and work seldom look more gloomy and disheartening than they do to a student of that ancient University of which the writer is an unworthy son, when he gets up in darkness and cold and hurricane; and hastens through mud and sleet along the gloomy streets to the lecture at half-past seven.

One happy result follows. During all the remainder of his life, the man who for three long winters in succession, each beginning about the twenty-eighth of October, and reaching on till the end of April, has undergone that discipline, can never cease to have a special feeling of thankfulness when on a morning of late October or early November he awakes at half-past five in the morning, and hears the rain outside; and then reflects that he need not get up and go out. The remembrance of many mornings past may send a chill through his frame; and various worries and cares which must be faced at rising may painfully suggest themselves; yet at least there is not that dismal rising before he has gathered heart to face the dreary day.

Things which were very far from pleasant when they occurred, are sometimes very pleasant to look back on. I remember well how through months of over-work at College, anything but enjoyable while they passed over, I kept written on a piece of paper, always before my eyes, Virgil's line which says so. I can see it yet, in large letters on my table; I used to look at it, in the silent house, at half-past three in the morning before going to bed, and to repeat it over when getting up wearily at half-past six again. *Forsitan olim hæc meminisse juvabit:* which was the graceful classic way of saying that there is a good time coming, and of advising sensible folk to wait a little longer. That time has come to the writer, and to many of his friends. We like to talk, when we meet, of the old days with their dismal mornings. It rejoiced me, between five and six this morning, to remember these things, and to feel the force of the anniversary. And now, when a new generation is gathering, on this very day, within the gloomy courts so well remembered, the recollection does no worse than call up in the writer many thoughts of the varied ways in which men take to work again. Suffer me to say here, my friendly reader, May the City and the University flourish together; according to the simple and straightforward wish of the pious burghers who first inscribed the motto on the scutcheon of the ancient town. And let me confess that I have already grown so old, that not without a certain mist that dims one's eyes, I can look on the crowd of lads and boys (for most of them are no more) in the Hall on the day of the opening of a session. You look back yourself, my friend; and from a record, not far to seek, you are able to discern a little of the mistakes, the follies, the repentances, the humiliations, the mortifications, the labors, the manifold takings-down, which await those hopeful young fellows, before they are battered, rudely enough, into trim for sober life. The Duke of Wellington said that all war was a series of blunders; it is not too much to say that blunders and repentances make up great part of the career of every mortal, especially in the days when he begins first to think for himself.

The winter session, which is the only one of the year in that University which is not to be named here, begins, as has been said, about the twenty-seventh or twenty-eighth of October. The vacation has lasted since the first of the preceding May. It need not be said that, to the more industrious students, that long vacation is in great part given to diligent study; yet it is always study to which your own sense of duty fixes the times and limits. *Now*, you begin to be under authority, and to have your task allotted to you from day to day. And at this season, it is a curious thing to come from the country to that city. You pass at a step from autumn, still rich with color, into winter, gloomy and gray. In an inland country region, late October is often a charming time; and the landscape has its own touching and even glowing beauty. Though many leaves have fallen, and make a dry rustle under your feet as you go through woodland ways, yet many of the trees are thickly clad: some wonderfully green; some touched by decay into beauty and glory, in the still sunshine of those beautiful days that come. And the dahlias and hollyhocks are blazing; for, as the season advances, the colors of nature deepen; and the pale and delicate hues of the early snowdrops, primroses, and lilies pass through the gradation of summer blossoms and roses into the glow of the late autumn flowers. It is as gentle maidenhood passes into blooming matronhood, with all its qualities more pronounced. And coming away from the country, at such a season, I dare say you have thought it still looking almost its best. But all these things are not, in the great city of that ancient University. The leaves are gone; all the country round is bare and bleak. The College-gardens, large and black-looking, are the most dismal scene that ever bore the pleasant name. You will find no winding walks through thick masses of evergreens, which in winter rain or winter frost look so lifelike and warm and cheering. The trees, poor and stunted, are all deciduous; and their leaves are not merely capable of falling, but have fallen in fact. The air is thick, and smoke abounds, — the smoke that makes the wealth of that wealthy city. And though you may be willing enough to set to work, and indeed rather weary of idleness or desultory study for some weeks past, you will probably confess that, even apart from the dismal lectures at half-past seven in the morning, it is rather a sad setting to work again.

Let us be thankful, my friend, if our work be such, that, after some escape from it, we can take to it again cheerfully and willingly. When we read in the newspapers about the reassembling of Parliament, the general effect conveyed to one's mind is a pleasant one. The impression left with us is that the members come back to their work willingly; they have been free from it so long that the appetite for the kind of thing has revived; and each man rises that morning with a positive feeling of exhilaration as he looks on to the event of the day. It is not as it was with Napoleon, even when he was Emperor. You remember how he enjoyed his Saturday and Sunday in the country quiet; and how on Sunday night he was accustomed to say, thinking of his return next morning to Paris and the cares of state, "To-morrow I must put on the yoke of misery again." Many people, young and old, feel as Napoleon felt. There is the heart-sinking of the nervous little boy, going back to school after the holidays, with vague fears of evil. There is the apprehension of a great mercantile man, entering upon a season in which he foresees many painful difficulties and complications, and does not know how things may turn out. It is as with the little bark, which, from a sheltered nook where it was lying snug and safe, puts out unwillingly into the full fury of winds and waves. And even coming back to work which you like, and to which you thankfully feel yourself in some degree equal, there is a certain shrinking from putting the shoulder to the collar again, and going stoutly at your task. There is a certain inertia, a certain nervous timidity to be overcome. You would like to quietly sit still where you are, and hide your head in a hole.

You will feel this, I think, in coming back from your autumn holiday-time; especially if you live and work in town. Human beings are never content. When you lived entirely in the country, it is very likely you used to think how pleasant and cheerful it would be to spend the dead months of the year in town; and just as the season is darkening down to winter, and the country beginning to look bleak and desolate, to get in among the warm dwellings and multitudes of your fellow-men. But now, if your home be in the city, you probably think, about this season, how enjoyable a thing it is to stay on in the country still, watching the stages through which it passes into its winter aspect; feeling the weather so much nearer you, and so much a greater part of your life, than it is in the town; looking for the days of the Martinmas summer, beautiful as any in all the year; waiting for the exhilaration of the frost, and the silence of the snow; and finding a value in the dreariest aspect of fields and hills and roads, for the hearty thankfulness with which it teaches you to enjoy the warm fireside, and light and books and music. It is October that gathers many men into town to work again, the yearly holidays over. And if you be a working man, who must earn your family's support by your labor, you may be pleased if you have had six weeks or two months of rest. If you have been away from work during the chief part of August and September, Nemesis might well be angry if you were to complain of coming back now as a hardship. Still you shrink a little. Nobody quite enjoys the idea of setting to work again; unless, indeed, his vacation have been so long that it has ceased to be enjoyed as rest, and come to be felt merely as the misery of idleness.

I suppose it is in human nature, that, after living for a while in a pleasant place, you should shrink from leaving it: many people find it costs them a painful effort to go away from their home; but, once away, they can quite easily stay away a long time. Inertia is unquestionably a property of mind as well as of matter. We don't like to move. Likely enough, my friend, in the autumn of this year, we have each been in half a dozen places, in any one of which we should have been content to have stayed all our days. And though no one can be fonder of his duty than yourself, my friend, or more pleased with the place where God has cast your lot; though it was a great strain and exertion to you to go away from both; yet it was a considerable strain and exertion to rise and come back.

Yes, it is a curious feeling you have, in coming away from any place which has been your home for even a short time; and there are not many things, besides actual physical pain, to which it does not cost a little pang to say Good-by. The thoughtful reader has probably remarked how different a place looks when you are coming away from it, from what it ever looked before. You observe, almost with a start, a great many little things and relations of things about it, which you never previously observed. All the familiar objects seem dumbly asking you to stay. And you must know the feeling by your own experience before you can rightly understand it. You cannot evolve it, *à priori*, out of your own consciousness. You may try to imagine what it would be like; but you cannot. Well does this writer remember how, in the days when he was a country clergyman, he used sometimes to pace up and down a certain little walk, every shrub by whose side had the look of an old friend; and to wonder what the feeling would be, and what the place would look like, if he should ever go away from it. But in those days he never thought he would; and his imagination would not serve him. And when the day, vaguely anticipated, came at last, every familiar holly and yew wore a new face; and the aspect of the whole scene was one never beheld before. In a lesser degree, but still a very appreciable degree, you feel all this in quitting a place where you have been staying for even six weeks. And you will be aware of a certain cheerlessness and desolateness, till your roots, thus torn up, get buried anew in the earth of your familiar home and its interests. Once fairly amid your own belongings and duties again, and you are all right. Your home seemed misty and unsubstantial while you were far away from it; but here it is again, real and warm, and with a general look of not unpleased recognition. And if you and I, my reader, in any degree deserve them, some kind looks and words of welcome, in the first busy days of somewhat confused occupation, may probably warm and cheer our spirit, and make us set with all the more hope and heart to work again.

There is no pleasanter incident in the little history of this time of return to very arduous duty, than the sending out of these Essays, which have been written in months past, as some not unsalutary change of occupation from graver thoughts and labors. The writer trusts that they may fall into the right hands. Certain volumes, which the friendly reader may know, have done so; and have gained for the writer the approval of various wise and good men, whose approval is to him among the most prized of earthly possessions. If these pages should fall into the hands of the man they do not suit, I hope he will not take the trouble of reading them; he has but to close the volume, and they will worry him no more. But the people for whom the author writes will understand easily that these chapters contain thoughts which are not unconsidered, and which aim at something beyond the mere amusement of a vacant hour.

In closing a former volume, I said I hoped the chapters it contained might not be the last. And now I am very pleased and thankful that the wish has been indulged. It is but a little part of a life, devoted to the most solemn and the happiest of all work, that has been spared to these Essays. But they have found an audience vastly wider than the writer's voice could reach, or than will ever listen to his sermons. And believing what I like to believe, not in self-conceit, but in thankfulness, I receive and cherish the assurance of very many who have told me that the reading of these pages did some little good to them; as the writing of these pages has done some little good to myself.

CHAPTER II.

CONCERNING ATMOSPHERES;

WITH SOME THOUGHTS ON CURRENTS.

I AM not going to write an essay on Ventilation, important as that subject unquestionably is; nor am I about to enter into any discussion of the various elements of which the air we breathe is made up. I am aware, indeed, that for the maintenance of animal and intellectual energy in their best state, it is expedient that the atmosphere should contain a certain amount of ozone; but what ozone is I do not know, and neither, I believe, does any one else. And on the matter of material currents, whether ocean currents, atmospheric currents, or river currents, I am not competent to afford the scientific reader much information. I know, indeed, as most people know, that it is well for Britain that the warm Gulf Stream sets upon our shores. I read in the newspapers how bottles thrown into the sea turn up in distant and surprising places. I am aware that the Trade Winds blow steadily from west to east.

And I have sat tranquilly, and looked intently at the onward flow of streams; from the slow and smooth canal-like river that silently steals on through the rich level English landscape, to the wild Highland torrent that tears down its rocky bed, in white foam and thunder.

But what I wish, my reader, that you and I should do at present, is to take a large view of the case, not needing any special knowledge of physical science. Let us remember just this, that the atmosphere in which we live is something that touches and affects us at every inch of our superficies, and at every moment of our life. It is not to say merely that we breathe it; but that it exerts upon every part of us, inner and outer, an influence which never ceases, and which, though possibly not much marked at the time, produces in the long run a very great and decided effect. You draw in the air from ague-laden fens, and you do not find anything very particular in each breath you draw. But breathe *that*, and live in *that*, for a few weeks or months, and see what will come to you. Or you go in the autumn, weak and weary with the season's work and worry, jaded and nervous, to the sea-side, and the bracing atmosphere in a little while insensibly does its work; your limbs grow strong and active again, and your mind grows energetic and hopeful. And you have doubtless felt for yourself how the heavy, smoky air of a large city makes you dull and stupid, and how the sparkling draughts you draw in of the keen, unbreathed air of the mountains, exhilarate and nerve anew. And as for currents, without going into details, we know this general fact: If you cast a floating thing upon a current, it will insensibly go along with the current. There may not be a stronger or a more perceptible push at one moment than at another; but there is an influence which in the main is unceasing, and there is a general drifting away. Slowly, slowly, the log cast into the sea, out in the middle of the Atlantic, comes eastward, week by week, till it is thrown somewhere on the outer coast of Ireland or of the Hebrides. And when the thing cast upon the current is more energetic than a log, still the current affects it none the less really. The Mississippi steamer breasts that great turbid stream, and makes way against it; but it makes way slowly. Let the engines cease to work, and the steamer drifts as the log drifted. Or let the engines work as before, and the vessel's head be turned down the stream; and then, going with the current, its speed is doubled.

Now, the atmosphere I mean in this essay is the atmosphere in which the soul lives and breathes; and the currents, those which carry along the moral and spiritual nature to developments better or worse. Shall we say it, for the most part to worse? In this world, in a moral sense, we generally drift towards evil, if we drift at all. You must warp up the stream if you would advance towards good. It seems to be God's purpose that anything good must be attained by effort: if you slothfully go with the current, it will be only to ill.

I am not able, just now, to give you a definition of either moral atmospheres or moral currents which satisfies me. You will gradually see my meaning, if you do not see it yet. Let it be said, generally, that to follow inclination within, or to yield to the vague influence of the things and people around you, is to drift with the moral current. And sensitively to feel the moral influences amid which you live — the moral influences arising from external nature, or from the dwelling in which you live, or from the people with whom you associate, or from the books and newspapers and magazines and reviews you read — is to feel the moral atmosphere. And a very great part of the influence which moulds human character, and decides human destiny, is of this vague, yet pervading kind. A tree, I am told, draws the chief part of its nourishment from the air, — very much more than it draws from the earth through its roots. The tree must have roots, or it would not live or grow at all; yet the multitude of leaves draw in *that* by which it mainly lives and grows. And it seems to me to be so with human beings. We must be morally rooted and grounded, as it were, by direct education, and by directly getting principles fixed in our minds. But after this is done, we mainly take our tone from the moral atmosphere. We are mainly affected by moral currents; and just as really when we strive against them as when we yield to them.

I am sure you know that a great many of the things we read — books, periodicals, and the like — affect us not so much by the ideas they convey, as by the general atmosphere with which they surround us. If you read, week by week, a clever, polished, cynical, heartless publication, it will do you harm insensibly; it will mould and color your ways of thinking and feeling much more than you would think. You like its talent, you know: but you disapprove, sometimes very keenly, its general character and tone; and you think you are so on your guard against these, inwardly protesting against them each time you feel them, that no effect will be produced by them upon you. You are mistaken in thinking so. You breathe and live in a moral atmosphere, which is quite sure to tell on you. You are cast on a current; and it needs constant pulling against it to keep you from drifting with it. And your moral nature is not (so to speak) ever on the stretch with the oars; ever in an attitude of resistance to the malaria. Yes; that clever, heartless, cynical paper will leave its impress on you by degrees. And on the other side, you know that the influence of writings which are not obtrusively instructive, may sink gently into our nature and do us much good. There is not much formal teaching in them; but as you read them, you feel you are breathing a general healthy atmosphere; you are aware of a quiet but decided and powerful current, setting steadily towards what is good and magnanimous and true.

No doubt, friendly reader, you feel that what I have said is just. In talking to people, in living in places, in reading books, you feel the atmosphere; you are aware of the current. I do not speak to people whose moral nature is callous as the hide of the rhinoceros, and who never feel the moral atmosphere at all. You might endeavor to prick a rhinoceros with a pin for some time without awaking any sensation in that animal. And there are human beings who, it is quite evident from their conversation and their doings on various occasions, are as little sensitive to the moral atmosphere, and the laws and proprieties which arise out of it, as the rhinoceros is to the very bluntest pin. They are not aware of any influence weaker than a physical push; as you remember the man who would take no hint less marked than a kicking. But *you* know, my friend, that in talking to different people, you insensibly take your tone from them; and you talk in a way accommodated to the particular case. There are people to whom, unawares, and without purpose prepense, you find yourself talking in a loud, lively manner, which is far from your usual one. There are others to whom you insensibly speak in a quiet, thoughtful way. And you cannot help this; it is just that you feel the atmosphere, and yield to it. It is as when you go out on a crisp frosty day, and without any special intention to that effect, find yourself walking smartly and briskly along. But if it be a still, sunshiny October afternoon, amid the brown and golden woods, you will unconsciously accommodate yourself to the surroundings: you will (if there be no special call for haste) walk pensively and slow. Now, some may unjustly fancy, as they remark how different your demeanor is in the society of different people, that you are an impostor, — a hypocrite, — not to say a humbug; that you are falsely assuming a manner foreign to your own, that you may suit the different people with whom you converse. It is not so. There is no design in what you do. You are not desiring to please the loud man by assuming a loud manner, reflecting his; as I have heard of some one who was regarded as having paid a delicate but effective compliment to a great man who wore a very odd waistcoat, by presenting himself in the presence of the great man, clad in a waistcoat exactly like his own. There is nothing of that kind; nothing insincere; nothing flunkeyish. It is only that you have a sensitive nature, which feels the atmosphere in which it is placed for the time. You know how mercury in frost feels the cold, and shrinks; it cannot help it. Then in warm weather it expands by the necessity of its nature. It always appeared to me in my childhood that Dr. Watts effectually justifies the most offensive deportment on the part of dogs, by suggesting that it is their Maker's intention they they should exhibit such a deportment. There is a passage, not much known, in a lyric by that poet, which runs to the effect: "Let dogs delight to bark and bite, for God has made them so." If the fact be admitted, the principle is sound; but as judicious discipline can greatly diminish the tendency of these animals to bark and bite, I doubt whether the words of Dr. Watts are to be construed in their full meaning. But there can be no question that mercury, which is a substance not accessible to moral considerations, deserves neither blame nor praise for expanding and shrinking according to its nature. And while I admit that any doings of human beings, partaking of a moral element, are (in the main) so under the control of the will, that the human beings may justly be held responsible for them, I hold that this sensitiveness to the moral atmosphere is very much a matter of original constitution, and that the man who feels it may fairly plead that his Maker "made him so." And very many people — shall we say the most exquisitely constituted of the race? — discern the moral atmosphere which surrounds some men by a delicate and unerring intuition. There are men who bring with them a frosty atmosphere; there are men who bring a sunshiny. You know people whose stiffness of manner freezes up the frankest and most genial. You know there are people to whom you would no more think of talking of the things which interest you most, than you would think of talking to a horse; or, let us say, to a donkey. Do you suppose that I should show my marked copy of *In Memoriam* to either my friend Dr. Log, or my friend Mr. Snarling?

I dare say some of my readers, going to see an acquaintance, have walked into his study, and found themselves, physically, in a choky, confined, hot-house atmosphere. And on entering into conversation with the man in the study they have found, morally, the same thing repeated. The moral atmosphere was just the physical over again. You remember the morbid views, the uncharitable judgments, the despondency of tone. And I think your inward exclamation was, Oh, for fresh air, physically and morally! And, indeed, I can hardly believe that sound and healthy judgments are ever come to, or that manly and truthful thoughts are produced, except when the physical atmosphere is pure and healthful. I would not attach much importance to the vote, upon some grave matter of principle, which is come to by an excited mob of even educated men, at four o'clock in the morning, in an atmosphere so thoroughly pestilential that it might knock a man down. And there are houses, on entering which you feel directly the peculiar moral atmosphere. It is oppressive. It catches your throat; it gets into your lungs; it (morally) puts a bad taste into your mouth. There are dwellings which, even in a physical sense, seem never to have fresh air thoroughly admitted; never to have the lurking malaria that hangs in corners and about window-curtains thoroughly cleared out, and the pure fresh air of heaven let in to fill every inch of space. There are more dwellings where this is so in a moral sense. You enter such a dwelling; you talk to the people in it. You at once feel oppressed. You feel stupid; worse than that, you feel sore and cantankerous. You feel you are growing low-minded. Anything like magnanimity or generosity goes out of you. You listen to wretched sneers against everything that is good or elevating. You find a series of miserable little doings and misdoings dwelt upon with weary iteration and bitter exaggeration. You hear base motives suggested as having really prompted the best people you know to their best doings. Did you ever spend an evening in the society of a cynical, sneering man, with some measure of talent and energy? You remember how you heard anything noble or disinterested laughed at; how you heard selfish motives ascribed to everybody; how some degrading association was linked with everything pure and excellent. Did you not feel deteriorated by that evening? Did you not feel that (morally) you were breathing the atmosphere of a sewer or a pigsty? And even when the atmosphere was not so bad as that, you have known the houses of really excellent folk, which were pervaded by such a stiffness, such an unnatural repression of all natural feeling, such a sense of constraint of soul, that when you fairly got out of the house at last, you would have liked to express your relief, and to give way to your pent-up energies, by wildly dancing on the pavement before the door like a Red Indian. And, indeed, you might very probably have done so, but for the dread of the police; and for the fear that, even through the dark, you might be discerned by the eyes of Mrs. Grundy.

Some people are so energetic and so much in ear nest, that they diffuse about them an atmosphere which is keenly felt by most men. And it often happens that you are very much affected by the moral influence of people, from almost all whose opinions you differ. I have no doubt that human beings who differ from Dr. Arnold and Mr. Hughes on almost every point of belief, have been greatly influenced, and influenced for the better, by these good men. There is something in the atmosphere that breathes from both of them that tends to higher and purer ways of thinking and feeling; that tends to make you act more constantly from principle, and to make you feel the solemnity of this life. And without supposing any special good fortune in the case of the reader, I may take for granted that you have known two or three persons whose presence you felt like a constant rebuke to anything mean or wrong in thought or deed, and like a constant stimulus to things good and worthy. You have known people, in the atmosphere of whose influence the evil in your nature seemed cowed and abashed. It seemed to die out like a nettle in frost; that clear, brisk, healthy atmosphere seemed to kill it. And you may have known men, after reading whose pages, or listening to whose talk, you felt more of kindly charity towards all your brethren in the helplessness and sinfulness of humanity. Of course, to diffuse a powerful influence, whether towards evil or good, a man must possess great force and earnestness of character. Ordinary mortals are like the chameleon, which takes something of the color of any strong-colored object it is placed near. They take their tone very much from the more energetic folk with whom they are placed in contact. I dare say you have known a man who powerfully influences for good the whole circle of men that surrounds him. Such a one must have a vast stock of vital and moral energy. Most people are like the electric eel, very much exhausted after having given forth their influence. A few are like an electric battery, of resources so vast that it can be pouring out its energy without cease. There are certain physical characteristics which often, though not always, go with this moral characteristic. It is generally found in connection with a loud, manly voice, a burly figure, a very frank address. Not always, indeed; there have been puny, shrinking, silent men, who mightily swayed their fellow-men, whether to evil or to good. But in the presence of the stronger physical nature, you feel something tending to make you feel cheerful, hopeful, energetic. I have known men who seemed always surrounded by a healthy, bracing atmosphere. When with such, I defy you to feel down-hearted, or desponding, or slothful. They put new energy, hopefulness, and life into you. Yes, my reader, perhaps you have found it for yourself, that to gain the friendship of even one energetic, thoughtful, good man, may suffice to give a new and healthier tone to your whole life. Yes, the influence of such a one may insensibly reach through all you think, feel, and do; as the material atmosphere pervades all material things. And such an influence may be exerted either through a fiery energy, or by an undefinable, gentle fascination. I believe that most men felt the first of these, who knew much of Dr. Chalmers. I believe that many have felt the second of these, in their intercourse with Dr. Newman or Mr. Jowett. Possibly, we might classify mankind under two divisions: the little band whose pith or whose fascination is such that they give the tone, good or bad; that they diffuse the atmosphere; and the larger host, whose soul is receptive rather than diffusive; the great multitude of human beings who take the tone, feel the atmosphere, and go with the current. It is probable that a third class ought to be added, including those who never felt anything, particularly, at all.

When you first enter a new moral atmosphere, you feel it very keenly. But you grow less sensitive to it daily, as you become accustomed to it. It may be producing its moral effect as really; but you are not so much aware of its presence. Did you ever go to a place new to you, of very unusual and striking aspect; and did you wonder if people there lived just as they do in the commonplace scenes amid which you live? Let me confess that I cannot look at the pictures of the quaint old towns of Belgium, without vaguely asking myself that question. In a lesser degree, the fancy steals in, even as one walks the streets of Oxford or of Chester. You feel how fresh and marked an atmosphere you breathe, in a visit of a few days' length to either town. But of course, if you live in the strangest place for a long time, you will find that life there is very much what life is elsewhere. I have often thought that I should like to do my in-door work in a room whose window opened upon the sea; so close to the sea that looking out you might have the waves lapping on the rock fifteen feet below you; and that when you threw the window up, the salt breeze might come into the chamber, a little feverish perhaps with several toiling hours. Surely, I think, some influence from the scene would mingle itself with all that one's mind would there produce. And it would be curious to look out, before going to bed, far over the level surface in the moonlight: to see the spectral sails passing in the distance; and to hear the never-ceasing sound, old as Creation. I do not know that the reader will sympathize with me; but I should like very much to live for a week or two at the Eddystone Light-house. There would be a delightful sense of quiet. There would be no worry. There would be plenty of time to think. It would be absolutely certain that the door-bell would never ring. And though there would be but limited space for exercise, there would unquestionably be the freshest and purest of air. No doubt if the wind rose at evening, you might through the night feel the light-house vibrate with the blow of the waves; but you could recall all you had read of the magnificent engineering of Smeaton; and feel no more than the slight sense of danger which adds a zest. I am aware that in a little while one would get accustomed to the whole mode of life. The flavor of all things goes with custom. When you go back to the sea-side, how salt the breeze tastes, which you never remarked while you were living there! And sometimes, looking back, you will wish you could revive the freshness and vividness of first impressions.

We have been thinking of the atmosphere diffused by books and by persons; let it be said that the thing about a book which affects your mind and character most, is not its views or arguments; it is its atmosphere. And it is so also with persons. It is not what people expressly advise you that really sways you; it is the general influence that breathes from all their life. A book may, for instance, set out sound religious views; but in such a hard cold way that the book will repel from religion. That is to say, the arguments may push one way, and the atmosphere the opposite way; and the atmosphere will neutralize the arguments and something more. And you will find people, too, whose advices and counsels are good; who often counsel their children or their friends to duty, and to earnestness in religion: but who neutralize and reverse the bearing of all these good counsels by the entire tone of their life. The words of some people say, Choose the good part, Ask for the best of all guidance and influence day by day; but their atmosphere says, Anything for money, — for social standing, — for spitefulness, — for general unpleasantness. You will find various Pharisees nowadays who loudly exclaim, "God be merciful to me a sinner;" but woe betide you, if you venture to hint to such that anything they can do is wrong!

Let me say, that you may read and you may hear religious instruction, which without asserting anything expressly wrong, still deteriorates you. It lowers you; you are the worse for it. There is an undefinable, but strongly-felt lack of the Christian spirit about it. Its views are mainly right; but somehow its atmosphere is wrong. I do not say this in any narrow spirit: it is not against one party of religionists more than another that I should bring this charge. Perhaps the teaching which is soundest in doctrine, is sometimes the most useless, through its want of the true Christian life; or through merely giving you the metaphysics of Christianity, without any real bringing of the vital truths of Christianity home to the heart, and to the actual case of those to whom they are told. I have read a book, — a polished, scholarly tale, the leading character in which was a clergyman — but in reading the book you felt a strong smack of heathenism. I do not mean the savage, cannibal heathenism which still exists in the islands of the South Pacific; but the polished heathenism which was many centuries since in Greece and Rome. The clergyman was sound in dogma, I dare say, if you had asked him for a confession of his faith; but his Christianity was an outside garment, while his whole nature was saturated with the old literature and mythology of that ancient day. Then you may find a book, a religious book, containing nothing on which you could well put your finger as wrong: yet you were left with a general impression of scepticism. *That* was the atmosphere. The views and arguments are as the solid ground: but you touch the solid ground but at a single point; — the circumambient ether is all around you, and within you. I have read pages setting out somewhat sad and discouraging views; yet as you turned the pages, you were aware of a general atmosphere of hopefulness and energy. And I have listened to what might have made pages, if it had been printed (pages which assuredly I should not have read), setting out the sublimest and most glorious hopes of humanity, in a way so dreary, dull, wearisome, and stupid, that the atmosphere was most depressing. You felt as though you were environed by a damp, thick fog.

It would be an endless task to reckon up the moral atmospheres in which human beings live; or even the moral atmospheres which you yourself, my friend, have breathed. But there are some that one remembers vividly; they did not come often enough, or continue long enough, to lose their freshness. Such is the atmosphere which surrounds all operations relating to the sale and purchase of horses. You remember how, when you went to buy one of those noble animals, you found yourself surrounded by a new and strongly-flavored phase of life. Was there not a general atmosphere as of swindling? You were surprised to hear lies, the grossest, told, even though they were sure to be instantly detected. You felt that your ignorance and capacity of being cheated were being gauged with great skill. It is a singular thing, indeed, that one of the most useful and beautiful of God's creatures should diffuse around him a most unhealthy moral atmosphere. You may have remarked that the noble steed is not merely surrounded by an ether filled with falsehoods; but that a less irritating, though still remarkable, ingredient, mingles with it, like ozone — it is the element of slang. I have remarked this with great interest, and mused much on it without succeeding in satisfactorily accounting for it. Why is it that to say a horse is a good horse should stamp you as a green hand; but that to say the animal is no bad nag, or a fairish style of hack, should convey the idea that you know various things? And wherefore should it be, that a shallow nature should be indicated by your saying you were willing to pay fifty pounds for the horse, while untold depth and craft shall be held to be implied by the statement that your tether was half a hundred?

A very disagreeable atmosphere, diffused by various persons, is that of suspicion. Some one has done you a kind turn, and your heart warms to the doer of it. But Mr. Snarling comes in; and you tell him, in hearty tones, of the kind turn, and of your warm feeling towards the man that did it. Mr. Snarling doubts, hints, insinuates, suggests a deep and traitorous design under that kind act; perhaps succeeds in chilling or souring your warm feeling; till, on the withdrawal of the unhealthy atmosphere, your better nature gets the upperhand again. And when next you meet the kind, open face of the friend who did you the kind turn, your heart smites you as you think what a wicked suspicious creature you were while within the baleful atmosphere of Snarling. You have seen, I dare say, very shallow and empty individuals, who fancied that it made them look deep and knowing, to say that beggars, for the most part, live in great luxury, and have money in the bank. *That* may be so in rare cases; but I KNOW that the want of the poor is often very real. It comes, doubtless, in some measure, from their own sin or improvidence; and as, of course, you and I never do wrong, let us throw a very large stone at the poor creature who is starving to-day, because she took a full meal of bread and butter and tea four days since. I have heard a man, with great depth of look, state that a certain cripple known to me could walk quite well. I asked the man for his authority. He had none, but vague suspicion. I told the man, with some acerbity (which I do not at all regret), that I knew the poor man well, and that I knew he was as crippled as he seemed. It looks knowing to declare of some poor starved creature that he is more rogue than fool. Whenever you hear *that* said, my reader, always ask what is the precise charge intended to be conveyed, and ask the ground on which the charge is made. In most cases you will get no answer to the second question; in very many no intelligible answer to the first. It would be a pleasant world to live in, if the people who dwell in it were such as they are represented by several persons known to me. I remember an outspoken old Scotch lady, to whom I was offering some Christian comfort after a great loss. I remember how she said, with a look as if she meant it, "If I did not believe all *that*, I should take a knife and cut my throat!" It was an honest confession of her faith, though made in unusually energetic terms. And I might say for myself, if I had not some faith in my race, it would be better to be off to the wilderness at once, or, like Timon, to the desolate shore. The wants of beggars, even of the least deserving, are, for the most part, very real. As for their luxuries, they are generally tea and buttered toast. Sometimes fried ham may also be found. Poor creatures! These things are the only enjoyments they have; and I, for one, am not ready with my anathema maranatha. I have known very suspicious and uncharitable persons who were extremely fat; doubtless they lived entirely on parched peas. And *all* the sufferings of the poor are not shams, paraded to the end of obtaining pence. I look back now, over a good many years, to the time when I was a youth at college. I remember coming home one night, between eleven and twelve o'clock, along a quiet street in a certain great city. I remember two poor girls standing in the shelter of the wall of a house, leaning against the wall, from the drenching rain. Neither noticed me. I see yet the deadly white face of one, — the haggard, sick look, as she crouched by the wall, and leant on the other's shoulder, as if just recovering from a faint. I hear yet the anxious, despairing voice with which the other said to her, "Are you better now?" The words were not spoken at me, or spoken for the ear of any passer-by. All this was on the dark midnight street, amid the drenching rain. It was a little thing; but it brought home to one the suffering that is quietly undergone in thousands of places over Europe each day and night.

Probably you have known people who were placed in a sphere where the atmosphere, moral and physical, was awfully depressing. They did their work poorly enough; and many blamed them severely. For myself, I was inclined to wonder that they did so well. Who could be a good preacher in certain churches of which I have known? I think there are few men more sensitive to the moral atmosphere than the preacher. There are churches in which there is a hearty atmosphere; others, in which there is a chilly atmosphere; others, with a bitter, narrow-minded, Pharisaic; others, with an atmosphere which combines the pragmatic, critical, and self-sufficient, with the densely stupid. But passing from this, I say that most men, even of those who do their work in life decently well, have only energy enough to do well if you give them a fair chance. And many have not a fair chance; some have no chance at all. There are human beings set in a moral atmosphere in which moral energy and alacrity could no more exist than physical life in the choke-damp of the mine. Be thankful, my friend, if you are placed in a fairly healthful atmosphere. You are doing fairly in it; but in a different one you might have pined and died. You are leading a quiet Christian life, free from great sin or shame. Well, be thankful; but do not be conceited; above all, do not be uncharitable to those for whom the race and the warfare have been too much.

I have said that it is the more energetic of the race that diffuse a moral atmosphere; the ordinary members of the race feel it. The energetic give the tone; the ordinary take it. There are minds whose nature is to give out; and minds whose nature is to take in.

But most men have energy enough, if rightly directed, to affect the air somewhat; and though the moral ingredient they yield may not be much in quantity, it may be able to supply just the precious ozone. Let us try to be like the sunshiny member of the family, who has the inestimable art to make all duty seem pleasant; all self-denial and exertion, easy and desirable; even disappointment not so blank and crushing; who is like a bracing, crisp, frosty atmosphere throughout the home, without a suspicion of the element that chills and pinches. You have known people within whose influence you felt cheerful, amiable, hopeful, equal to anything! Oh, for that blessed power, and for God's grace to exercise it rightly! I do not know a more enviable gift than the energy to sway others to good; to diffuse around us an atmosphere of cheerfulness, piety, truthfulness, generosity, magnanimity. It is not a matter of great talent; not entirely a matter of great energy; but rather of earnestness and honesty, — and of that quiet, constant energy which is like soft rain gently penetrating the soil. It is rather a grace than a gift; and we all know where all grace is to be had freely for the asking.

You see, my reader, I have spoken of atmospheres and currents together. For every moral atmosphere is of the nature of a moral current. As you breathe the atmosphere, you feel that there is an active force in it; that you are beginning to drift away. It is not merely a present sense of something that comes over you; but you know that it sets you floating onward to something beyond your present feeling. The more frequent tendency of a moral atmosphere is to assimilate your moral nature to itself. Perhaps all atmospheres, if you live in them long enough, tend to this. But there are some atmospheres which, just at first, are so very disagreeable, that their effect is repellent; they tend to make you wish to be just as different from themselves as you can. But the refined person, at first revolted by a rude and coarse atmosphere, will, in years, grow subdued to it; and the pure young soul, shocked and disgusted at the first approach of gross sin, comes at last to bear it and to exceed it. Yes, the ultimate tendency of all moral atmospheres upon all ordinary people, is to assimilate them to the element in which they live. Let men breathe any atmosphere long enough, and this will follow; save in the case of an exceptional man here and there. It is a very bad thing for a young person to be much among thoroughly worldly people, or among mere money-making people. Let us not cry down money; it is a great and powerful thing. You remember, it was not money, but the over love of money, that was "the root of all evil." But it is most unhappy to live among those from whose entire ways of thinking and talking you get the general impression, that money is the first and best thing; and that the great end of life is to obtain it; and that almost any means may be resorted to for that end.

All this is not said in so many words; but it pervades you unseen; you breathe it like an unwholesome malaria. You take it in, not merely at every breath, but at every pore. And the result of years of this is, that the warm-hearted, generous youth grows into the sordid, heartless old man; and that the enthusiastic young Christian is sometimes debased into a very chilly, lifeless, and worldly middle age.

And now, before I end, you must let me say this. And when I say it upon this page (which never formed any part of a sermon) you will know that I say it not because I think I must, but because I honestly believe it. There is a certain blessed influence which can mingle itself with every moral atmosphere that a human being can honestly breathe; and which can make every such atmosphere healthful. You know what I mean. It is the influence of that Holy Spirit, whose presence the Redeemer said was more valuable and profitable than even His own; and who is promised without reservation to all who heartily ask His presence. And you know, too, that we have a sure promise, that if we build on the right foundation, the current of our whole life will tend towards what is happy and good. There may be a little eddy backwards here and there, and sometimes what seems a pause, but it is in the direction of these things that the whole current sets; it is towards these that "all things work together." I firmly believe that the natural tendency of all moral currents, apart from God's grace, is downwards. Apart from *that*, we shall always grow worse; with it, we shall always grow better. Believe me, my reader, when I say, that if all our life and all our lot be not hallowed by the presence in all of the Blessed Spirit, we may be sure that we are breathing a moral atmosphere which wants just the precious ozone that is needful to true health and life. And if we have not, penitently and humbly, confided ourselves to our Saviour, we may know that we are drifting with a current which is certainly bearing us on towards all that is evil and all that is woful. It is sad to see the poor little pale and sickly children of some dark, stifling close in a large city; poor little things who never breathe the free country air; who are living in an unwholesome atmosphere within doors and without, in which they are pining, and growing up weak and nerveless; but it is more sad to see the immortal soul stunted, emaciated, and distorted, through the unhealthy moral air it breathes. It must have been a miserable sight, the little boat with the man in it asleep, drifting smoothly and swiftly along, beyond human reach, towards the tremendous cataract; but it is more miserable, if we saw it rightly, to see a human soul, in spiritual sleep, drifting day by day towards the fearful plunge into final woe. Let us pray, my reader, for both of us; that God would be with us by His Spirit, and keep us in all ways that we go; that in all our life we may breathe the Atmosphere of His presence; and by the Current of all our life be brought nearer to Himself!

CHAPTER III.

CONCERNING BEGINNINGS AND ENDS.

EVERYTHING in this world has a Beginning and an End.

After writing that sentence, which (as you see) sets forth a great general principle, I stopped for some time, to consider whether it holds always true. As one grows older, one grows always more cautious as to general principles. My young friend, when you are arguing any question with an acute opponent, you should, as a rule, never assent to any general principle which he may state. He may ask you, with an indignant air, Don't you admit that two and two make four? Let your answer be, No, I admit nothing, till I see how it touches the matter which concerns us at present. You do not know what may be involved in the admission sought; or what may follow from it. The most innocent-looking general principle may lead to the most appalling consequences. The general principle which appears most unquestionably true, may prove glaringly false in some very ordinary case. You should request time for consideration before you admit any axiom in morals, metaphysics, or politics; or you should ask your adversary what he means to build upon it, before you can say either yes or no to it. Do as the Scotch judges do when a difficult case has been argued before them. I discover from the newspapers that they are wont to say, that they will take such a case to *avizandum:* which I suppose (no one ever told me) means that they must think twice, or even oftener, before deciding a matter like *that.*

I have taken the general principle, already stated, to *avizandum.* It seems all right. But I remember, in thinking of it, at how great advantage a judge is placed, in trying to come to a sound decision. Very clever and well-informed men state the arguments on either side. And all the judge has to do, is to say which arguments seem to him the strongest. He has no fear that any have been overlooked. But a human being, weighing a general principle, must act as counsel on each side, as well as judge. He must call up before his mind, all that is to be said for and against it; as well as say whether the weightiest reasons make for or against. And he may quite overlook some important reason, on one side or other. He may quite forget something so obvious and familiar that a child might have remembered it. Or he may fail to discern that some consideration which mainly decides his judgment is open to a fatal objection, which every one can see is fatal the instant it is stated. Was it not Sir Isaac Newton, who had a pet cat and kitten? And did not these animals annoy him while busy in his study, by frequently expressing their desire to be let out and in? The happy thought struck him, that he might save himself the trouble of often rising to open his study-door for their passage, by providing a way that should always be practicable for their exit or entrance. And accordingly the great man cut in his door a large hole for the cat to go out and in, and a small hole for the kitten. He failed to remember, what the stupidest bumpkin would have remembered, that the large hole through which the cat passed might be made use of by the kitten too. And the illustrious philosopher discerned the error into which he had fallen, and the fatal objection to the principle on which he had acted, only when taught it by the logic of facts. Having provided the holes already mentioned, he waited with pride to see the creatures pass through them for the first time. And as they arose from the rug before the fire, where they had been lying, and evinced a disposition to roam to other scenes, the great mind stopped in some sublime calculation; the pen was laid down; and all but the greatest man watched them intently. They approached the door, and discerned the provision made for their comfort. The cat went through the door by the large hole provided for her; and instantly the kitten followed her THROUGH THE SAME HOLE! How the great man must have felt his error! There was no resisting the objection to the course he had pursued, that was brought forward by the act of the kitten. And it appears almost certain that if Newton, before committing himself by action, had argued the case; if he had stated the arguments in favor of the two holes; and if he had heard the housemaid on the other side; the error would have been averted. But then Newton had not the advantage which the Chancellor has; he had not the matter argued before him. He argued the matter on either side, for himself; and he overlooked a very obvious and irrefragable consideration.

You and I, my reader, have many a time done what was perfectly analogous to the doing of Sir Isaac Newton. We have formed opinions and expressed them; and we have done things, thinking we were doing wisely and right; just because we forgot something so plain that you would have said no mortal could forget it, — something which showed that the opinion was idiotic, and the doing that of a fool. You know, more particularly, how men who have committed great crimes, such as murder, seem by some infatuation to have been able to discern only the one obvious reason that seemed to make the commission of that crime a thing tending to their advantage; and to have been incapable of looking just a handbreadth farther on, so as to see the fatal, crushing objection to the course they took; — the absolute ruin and destruction that must of necessity follow. And the opinion of many men upon any subject may often be likened to a table which the art of the upholsterer has fashioned to stand upon a single leg. They hold the opinion for just one reason: and that reason an unsound one. Give that reason a blow with the fatal, unanswerable objection; down comes the opinion; even as down would come the table, whose single leg was knocked away.

I am well aware that the severe critic who has read the lines which have been written, may feel disposed to accuse the writer of a disposition to wander from his path. A great deal of what has been said, is as when you take a look over the stile at a footpath running away from the beaten highway you are to traverse; and end by getting over the stile, and walking a little way along the footpath; intending, no doubt, ultimately to return to the beaten highway, and to plod steadily along it. All this discussion of general principles ought to have been despatched in a line or two, analogous to the glance over the stile. But let the critic take into account the fact, that since the writer last sat down to write an essay, he has written a great many serious pages, which it cost hard work to write, and in which nothing in the nature of an intellectual frisk could be permitted. And thus it is, that with a great sense of relief, he finds himself writing a page whereon he may mildly disport himself; casting logical and other trammels aside; and enjoying a little mental recreation. And now, going back from the path, and getting over the stile, we are in the highway again. We turned out of the highway, you remember, at the point where it was said, that EVERYTHING IN THIS WORLD HAS A BEGINNING AND AN END; and that, upon reflection, it seemed that the general principle might be accepted as true. No doubt, in our early days, we have heard sermons which we thought would never end; yet ultimately, and after the expiration of long time, they did. And even those things within our recollection, which seem as exceptions to the great principle, are probably exceptions rather in appearance than in reality. I remember, indeed, an aged clergyman whom in my youth I occasionally heard preach; who always began the first sentence of his sermon, but who never ended it; at least not till the close of the sermon; and no human being could know when that sentence ended, or say at what point (if any point in particular) it ceased to be. Still even that first sentence of each discourse of that good man, came to a close somehow. It stopped, if it was not finished, — because the sermon stopped. So you see that even that indefinite sentence can hardly be regarded as an exception to the rule that all things in this world have a beginning and an end.

And now, my friend, having laid down the broad principle with which this dissertation sets out, let me proceed to say that it is one of the greatest blessings of this life, as well as one of the saddest things in this life, that there are such things as beginnings and ends.

We cannot bear a very long, uniform look-out. You may remember Miss Jane Taylor's pleasantly-told story concerning a certain clock. The pendulum of that clock began to calculate how often it would have to swing backwards and forwards in the week and the month to come; then, looking still farther into futurity, it calculated, by a pretty hard exercise of mental arithmetic, how often it would have to swing in a year. And it got so frightened at the awful prospect, that it determined at once to stop. There was something crushing in that long look-out. It was killing to take in at once that unvaried way; on, and on, and on. The pendulum forgot the blessed fact of beginnings and ends; forgot that to our feeling there are beginnings and ends even in the duration, the expanse, the employment, which in fact is most unvarying. It is an unspeakable blessing that we can stop, and start again, in everything; and that we can fancy we do so even when we do not. The pendulum was not afraid of a hundred beats, or of a thousand; but the prospect of millions terrified it. Yet millions are just an aggregate of many hundreds; and the pendulum could without fatigue do the hundred, and then set off again upon another hundred, and do that without fatigue. The journey that crushes us down when we contemplate it as one long weary thing can be borne when we divide it into stages. And one great lesson of practical wisdom is to train ourselves to mentally divide everything into stages; in short, to cling habitually to the invaluable doctrine and fact of beginnings and ends.

There was a poor cabman at Paris who committed suicide not long ago. He left behind him a letter explaining his reasons for the miserable deed. His letter expressed no violent feeling,—spoke of no great blow that had befallen him. It said that he ended his life because he was "weary of doing the same things over and over again every day." The poor man's mind was doubtless unhinged. Yet you see what he did, and how he nursed his insanity. He looked too far ahead. He saw all life as one expanse. He forgot that life is broken into many stages,—that it is made up of beginnings and endings. He could not bring himself, for the time, to see it so. Each separate day he might have stood; but a thousand days held in prospect at once beat him. It was as the bundle of rods was so impossible to break, though each single rod might easily enough be broken. It was the fallacy which tells so heavily upon most public speakers: that you stand in great awe of a crowd of a thousand or two thousand men, each of whom individually would inspire you with no awe at all.

Now, my readers, I know perfectly well that you have all known a feeling of weariness and almost of despair arise, when you looked far forward and saw the long weary way that seemed to stretch on and on before you in life. I believe that it is not so much what we are actually enduring at the time that prompts the cry, "Now, I can bear this no longer!" as some sudden, vivid glimpse of all this, lasting on, and on, and on. There are few lives in which it is not expedient to "take short views;" few minds that, without weariness and depression, can take in at one view any very great part of their life at once. Sometimes there comes on us the poor Frenchman's feeling: Here is this same round over, and over, and over; the occupations of each day are a circle, and we are just going round and round it, like a horse in a mill. To-morrow will be like to-day; and then to-morrow, and the day after that; and so on, on, on. The feeling is a morbid one, and a wrong one; but it is a common one. A little of the sea in a tumbler is colorless; but a vast deal of the sea, seen in its ocean bed, is green. With life the case is reversed. In the commonplace course of life, the path we are actually treading may look rather green, — green, I mean, like the cheerful verdure of grass; but if you take in too great a prospect, the whole tract is apt to take the aspect of a desert waste, with only a green spot here and there. You will not add to the cheerfulness and hopefulness of man or of child, by drilling into him: "This morning you will do such and such things; and all day such other things; and in the evening such other things; then you will sleep. To-morrow morning you will rise, and then the same things over and over; and so on, on. I have known a malignant person who enjoyed the work of presenting to others such disheartening views of life. Let me, my reader, counsel the opposite course. Let us not look too far on. Let us not look at life as one unvaried expanse; although we may justly do so. Let us discipline our minds to look at life as a series of beginnings and ends. It is a succession of stages; and we shall think of one stage at a time. "Sufficient unto the day is the evil thereof." Most people can bear one day's evil; the thing that breaks men down is the trying to bear on one day the evil of two days, twenty days, a hundred days. We can bear a day of pain, followed by a night of pain; and that again by a day of pain, and thus onward. But we can bear each day and night of pain only by taking each by itself. We can break each rod, but not the bundle. And the sufferer, in real great suffering, turns to the wall in blank despair when he looks too far on; and takes in a uniform dreary expanse of suffering, unrelieved by the blessed relief of even fanciful beginnings and ends.

I remember a poor woman whom I used often to visit and pray with, in my first parish. She died of cancer; and the excruciating disease took eight months to run its course, after having reached the point at which the pain became almost intolerable. In all that long time, the poor woman told me that she was never aware that she had slept; it seemed to her that the time never came in which she ceased to be conscious of agony. Her sufferings formed an unbroken duration, undivided by beginnings and ends. She was a good Christian woman, and had a blessed hope in another world. But I can never cease to remember her despairing face, as she seemed to look onward to weeks of agony, always growing worse and worse, till it should wear her down to her grave.

The power and habit of taking comprehensive views is not in every case a desirable thing. It is well for us that we should look at our work in life in its parts, rather than as a whole. Of course you understand what I mean. I am far from saying that we ought not oftentimes to consider what is the drift and bearing of all our life, and of all we are doing in it. I mean that to avoid a fatiguing and disheartening result, we should, for certain purposes, look not at the entire chain, but at each successive link of it. Of course, we know each link will be succeeded by the next; but let us think of them one at a time. Let us be thankful for Saturday night, and let us enjoy it; and let us hold at arm's length the intruding thought of Monday morning, when the shoulder must be put to the collar again. No doubt, in the work of life, every end is also a beginning. We rest for a little, perhaps only in thought and feeling; and then we go at our work again. But it is a convenient thing, and it helps to carry us on in our way, to mark out a number of successive ends, and thus to divide our journey into successive stages. It is well for us that when we start, we cannot see how far we have to go. We should give up all effort in despair, if from the beginning we held in view all the interminable length of way, whose length we shall hardly feel when we are wiled away along it gradually, step by step. It has always appeared to me extremely bad policy in any preacher, who desires to keep up the interest of his congregation, to announce at the beginning of the sermon, that in the first place he will do so and so ; and in the second place such another thing ; and in the third place something else ; and finally close with some practical remarks. I can say for myself, that whenever I hear any preacher say anything like that, an instant feeling of irksomeness and weariness possesses me. You cannot help thinking of the long tiresome way that is to be got over, before happily reaching the end. You check off each head of the sermon as it closes ; but your relief at thinking it is done, is dashed by the thought of what a deal more is yet to come. No : the skilful preacher will not thus map out his subject, telling his hearers so exactly what a long way they have to go. He will wile them along, step by step. He will never let them have a long out-look. Let each head of discourse be announced as it is arrived at. People can bear one at a time, who would break down in the simultaneous prospect of three, not to say of seven or eight. And then, when the sermon is nearly done, you may, in a sentence, give a connected view of all you have said ; and your skill will be shown if people think to themselves, what a long way they have been brought without the least sense of weariness. I lately heard a sermon, which was divided into seven heads. If the preacher had named them all at the beginning, the congregation would have ceased to listen ; or would have listened under the oppressive thought of what a vast deal awaited them before they would be free. But each head was announced just as it was arrived at ; the congregation was wiled along insensibly ; and the sermon was listened to with breathless attention from the first sentence to the last.

Let it be so with life, and the work of life. It would crush down any man's resolution, if he saw in one glance the whole enormous bulk of labor, which he will get through in a lifetime, without feeling it so very much at each successive stage. It is well to break up our journey into separate portions ; to take it bit by bit ; to set ourselves a number of successive ends ; even though we know that we are practising a sort of deception on ourselves ; and that when the end we have immediately in view is reached, our work will be just as far from being done, as ever. Your little boy has before him the mighty task of his education. You do not tell the little thing at once the whole extent of toil that is included in *that.* No ; you fix on a small part of the work that is to be done ; you show the little man *that* as his first end. *That* is the first thing to be done ; and then we shall see what is to come next. And yet you know, and the little child knows just as well, that after he has conquered that tremendous alphabet, he must just begin again with something else; that by a hundred steps, — each set out at first as an end to be attained; and each indeed an end, but likewise a beginning, — he must mount from his first little book onwards and upwards into the fields of knowledge and learning. Let us, if we are wise men, hold by the grand principle of STEP BY STEP; let us be thankful that God, knowing that weariness is a thing that must be felt at intervals by the minds and bodies of all His creatures, has appointed that they shall live in a world of Beginnings and Ends. Yes, we can stand a day at a time; but if we forget the law of beginnings and ends, we shall come to be bearing the weight of a hundred days together. And *that* will crush the strongest.

Many people, of an anxious temperament, are like the pendulum already mentioned. The pendulum looked ahead to the incalculable multitude of ticks, forgetting that there would always be a moment to tick in. And you can easily see that many human beings plod heavily and dully through their work in life, because instead of giving their mind mainly to the present tick, they are thinking of the innumerable ticks that are coming. You know quite well that the work of life is done by most animals that have to work, in a dull, spiritless way. Few go through their work in a cheerful, lively way. Even inferior animals are coming to imitate their rational fellow-creatures. The other day, I was driving in a cab along a certain broad and ugly highway, which unites Athens with the Piræus. I overtook and passed various drays, drawn by fine large horses. I carefully remarked the expression of the countenance of each successive horse. All of them had a very gloomy and melancholy look. They seemed as though they were enduring. They could stand it; and that was all. And I thought, here is an example of the way in which this world mainly goes on. It goes on; it gets through; but not cheerfully. You could know, even if you had no better means of knowing, that there is something wrong. And the working bees of the human race do, for the most part, go through their work like the dull, down-looking horse. The horses were plump and sleek; they were plainly well fed and well groomed; yet their expression was sorrowful, or at least apathetic. It would have struck you less, to have seen that dull look on the face of some poor, half-starved screw. And you know that it is generally the human beings whose material advantages are the greatest, who have the most unsatisfied and unhappy expression of countenance. Look at the portraits of cabinet ministers and the like. Few work with a light heart, and with enjoyment in their work. Many forebodings, and many cares, sit heavily upon the heart and brain of most. Oh for more practical belief in Beginnings and Ends!

It is characteristic of those things which possess a Beginning and an End, that they also possess a Middle, of greater or less extent. But we do not mind about the middle nearly so much. The middle is much less affecting and striking. It is the first start, and then the close, that we mainly feel. You know the peculiar interest with which we look at the setting sun of summer, in his last minutes above the horizon. Of course he was going on just as fast through all the day; but at mid-day, we did not know the value of each minute, as we do when he is fast going down. I have been touched by the sight of human life, ebbing almost visibly away; and you could not but think of the sun in his last little space above the mountains, or above the sea. I remember two old gentlemen, great friends; both on the extreme verge of life. One was above ninety; the other above eighty. But their wits were sound and clear; and, better still, their hearts were right. They confessed that they were no more than strangers and pilgrims on the earth; they declared plainly that they sought a country, far away, where most of those they had cared for were waiting for them. But the body was very nearly worn out; and though the face of each was pleasant to look at, paralysis had laid its grasp upon the aged machinery of limb and muscle which had played so long. I used, for a few weeks, to go one evening in the week and sit with them, and take tea. They always had tea in large breakfast cups; other cups would not have done. I remember how the two paralytic hands shook about, as they tried to drink their tea. There they were, the two old friends; they had been friends from boyhood, and they had been over the world together. You could not have looked, my friend, but with eyes somewhat wet, at the large tea-cups, shaking about, as the old men with difficulty raised them to their lips. And there was a thing that particularly struck me. There was a large old-fashioned watch, always on a little stand on the tea-table, ticking on and on. You seemed to feel it measuring out the last minutes, running fast away. It always awed me to look at it and hear it. Only for a few weeks did I thus visit those old friends, till one died; and the other soon followed him, where there are no palsied hands or aged hearts. No doubt, through all the years the old-fashioned watch had gone about in the old gentleman's pocket, life had been ebbing as really and as fast as then. And the sands were running as quickly for me as for the aged pilgrims. But then with me it was the middle; and to them it was the end. And I always felt it very solemn and touching, to look at the two old men on the confines of life, and at the watch loudly ticking off their last hours. One seemed to feel time ebbing, — as you see the setting sun go down.

Beginnings are difficult. It is very hard to begin rightly in a new work or office of any kind. And I am thinking not merely of the inertia to be overcome in taking to work; though that is a great fact. In writing a sermon or an essay, the first page is much the hardest. You know, it costs a locomotive engine a great effort to start its train; once the train is off, the engine keeps it going at great speed with a tenth, or less, of the first heavy pull. But I am thinking now of the many foolish things which you are sure to say and do in your ignorance, and in the novelty of the situation. Even a Lord Chancellor has behaved very absurdly in his first experience of his great elevation. It would be a great blessing to many men to be taken elsewhere, and have a fresh start. As a general rule, a clergyman should not stay all his life in his first parish. His parishioners will never forget the foolish things he did at his first coming, in his inexperienced youth. There, he cannot get over these; but elsewhere he would have the good of them, without the ill. He would have the experience, dearly bought; while the story of the blunders and troubles by which it was bought would be forgotten. I dare say there are people, miserable and useless where they are, who, if they could only get away to a new place, and begin again, would be all right. In that new place they would avoid the errors and follies by which they have made their present place too hot to hold them. Give them a new start; give them another chance; and taught by their experience of the scrapes and unhappiness into which they got by their hasty words, their ill temper, their suspicion and impatience, their domineering spirit, and their determination in little things to have their own way; you would find them do excellently. Yes, there is something admirable about a Beginning! There is something cheering to the poor fellow who has got the page on which he is writing hopelessly blotted and befouled, when you turn over a new leaf, and give him the fresh unsullied expanse to commence anew! It is like wiping out a debt that never can be paid, and that keeps the poor struggling head under water; but wipe it out, and oh, with what new life will the relieved man go through all his duty! It is a terrible thing to drag a lengthening chain; to know that, do what you may, the old blot remains, and cannot be got rid of. I know various people, soured, useless, and unhappy, who (I am sure) would be set right forever, if they could but be taken away from the muddle into which they have got themselves, and allowed to begin again somewhere else. I wish I were the patron of six livings in the Church. I think I could make something good and happy of six men who are turned to poor account now. But alas, that in many things there is no second chance! You take the wrong turning; and you are compelled to go on in it, long after you have found that it is wrong. You have made your bed, and you must lie on it. And it is sad to think how early in life all life may be marred. A mere boy or girl may get into the dismal lane which has no turning; and out of which they never can get, to start afresh in a better track. How many of us, my readers, would be infinitely better and happier, if we could but begin again!

An End is sometimes a very great blessing. I have no doubt, my readers, that in your childhood you have often felt this when a sermon was brought to a close. Perhaps in maturer years you have experienced a like emotion of relief under the like circumstances. I can say deliberately that never in my youth did I once wish that such a discourse should be longer than it was. Yet we all remember how we have shrunk from Ends. You may have read a fairy tale by Mr. Thackeray, with illustrations by its author. One of these is a cartoon, representing a boy eating a bun, apparently of superior quality; and at the same time expressing a sentiment common to early youth. He eats; and as he eats, he speaks as follows: "Oh what fun! Nice plum-bun! How I wish it never was done!" I remember the mental state. I have known it well. In my mind it is linked with the thought of plum-pudding, and of other luxuries and dainties. It was sad to see the object lessen, as it was enjoyed, — to see it melt away, like a summer sunset! And about Christmas-time, one had sometimes a like feeling as to the appetite and relish for plum-pudding and the like. Would it were unceasing! I mean the appetite. But you remember how it flagged. And though you stimulated it with cold water, yet the fourth supply beat you, and had to be taken away. And you remember, too, how you shrunk from the end of your holiday season, and wished that time would stand still. You may have read the awful scene in Christopher Marlowe's "Faustus," where the hapless philosopher, on the verge of his appointed season, seems to cling to each moment as it passes away from him. And oh, my reader, if the great work of life have not been done while the day lasted, think how awful it will be to feel that the end of the day of grace is here! Think of poor Queen Elizabeth in her dying hour, offering all the wealth of her kingdom for another day of life! We cannot, in the commonplace days of ordinary health and occupation, rightly realize the tremendous fact; but think of the End of this life, to the man who has no hope beyond it! To feel that all in the world you have toiled for and loved is going from you; to feel your feeble hand losing its grasp of all; to see the faces around grow dim through the mists of death; to feel the weary heart pausing, and the last chill creeping upwards; to feel that you are driven irresistibly to the edge of the awful gulf, — and no hope beyond! But remember, reader, it will be your own fault, if you come to *that.*

It is the end of a career that gives the character to it all. We feel as if a life, however honorable and happy, were blighted by a sorry ending. The thought of Napoleon at St. Helena squabbling about the thickness of his camp soup, and the number of clean shirts to be allowed him, casts back an impression of pettiness upon the man even in his mid-career. There is a graver consideration. If a man had lived many years in usefulness and honor, but finally fell into grievous sin and shame, we should think of his life as on the whole a shameful one. But if a man end his career nobly, if his last years are honorable and happy, we should think of his life on the whole as one of happiness and honor, though its beginning were ever so lowly and sad. You remember how a great king of ancient days asked a philosopher to name some of the happiest of the race. The philosopher named several men, all of whom were dead. The king asked him why he did not think of men still living; "Look at all my splendor," he said to the philosopher; "why do you not think of *me?*" "Ah," said the wise man; "who knows what your life and your lot may be yet? I call no man happy before he dies!" [Distinguished classical scholar, I am not telling the story for you.] And, sure enough, that monarch was reduced to captivity and misery; and died a miserable captive: and so you would not say that his life was a happy or a prosperous one on the whole. But in the most important of all our concerns, my friend, the End is far more important than that. You know that though the monarch, vanquished and uncrowned, died in a dungeon, *that* could not blot out the years of royalty he had actually lived. He had been a king, once; however fallen now. The man who sits by his lonely fireside, silent and deserted, can yet remember the days when that quiet dwelling was noisy and gladsome with young voices:

they were real days, when his children were round him; and it does him good yet to look back on them, — though now the little things are in their graves. But the fearful thing about the Christian who ends in sin and shame, is this: He dare not comfort himself under the present wretchedness, by looking back to better days, when he thought he was safe. The fearful thing is that this present end of sin has power to blot out those better days: if a man, however fair his profession, end at last manifestly not a Christian, this proves that he never was a Christian at all! You see what tremendous issues depend upon the Christian life ending well! It is little to say that ending ill is a sad thing at the time: it is that ending ill flings back a baleful light on all the days that went before! If the end be bad, then there was something amiss all along, however little suspected it may have been. It is only when the end is well over, that you can be perfectly sure you are safe. You remember Mr. Moultrie's beautiful poem, about his living children and his dead child. The living children were good, were all he could wish; but God only knew how temptation might prevail against them as years went on; but as for the dead one, *he* was safe. "It may be that the Tempter's wiles *their* souls from bliss may sever; But if our own poor faith fail not, *he* must be ours forever!" Yes, that little one had passed the End; no evil nor peril could touch *him* more.

I dare say you have sometimes found that for a lay or two, a line of poetry or some short sentence of prose would keep constantly recurring to your memory. I find it so; and the line is sometimes Shakspeare's; sometimes Tennyson's; often it is from a certain Volume (the Best Volume) of which it is my duty to think a great deal. And I remember how, not long since, for about a week, the line that was always recurring was one by Solomon, king and philosopher (and something more): it was "Better is the end of a thing than the beginning." And at first I thought that the words sounded sad, and more heathen-like than Christian. Has it come to this, that God's Word tells us concerning the life God gave us, that the best thing that can happen to us is soonest to get rid of that sad gift; and that each thing that comes our way, is something concerning which we may be glad when it is over? I thought of Mr. Kingsley, and wondered if the sum of the matter, after all, is "The sooner it's over, the sooner to sleep;" and of Sophocles, and how he said "Not to be, is best of all; but when one hath come to this world, then to return with quickest step to whence he came, is next." But then I saw, gradually, that the words are neither cynical nor hopeless; that they do but remind us of the great truth, that God would have our life here one of constant progress from good to better, and so the End best of all. We are to be "forgetting those things which are behind, and reaching forth unto those which are before," because the best things are still before us. If things in this world go as God intended they should, then everything is a step to something else, something farther: which ought to be an advance on what went before it; which ought to be better than what went before it. And above all, the End of our life here (if it end well), so safe and so happy, is far better than its Beginning, with all the perils of the voyage yet to come.

I thought of these things the other Sunday afternoon, seeing the Beginning and the End almost side by side. At that service I did not preach; and I was sitting in a square seat in a certain church, listening to a very good sermon preached by a friend. A certain little boy, just four years old, came and sat beside me, leaning his head on me as a pillow; and soon after the beginning of the sermon, the little man (very properly) fell sound asleep. And (attending to the sermon all the while) I could not but look down at the fat rosy little face, and the abundance of curly hair; the fresh, clear complexion, the cheerful, innocent expression; and think how fair and pleasing a thing is early youth, — how beautiful and hopeful is our life's Beginning. And after service was over, on my way home, I went to see a revered friend, who, at the end of a long Christian life, was dying. There was the worn, ghastly face, with its sharp features; the weary, worn-out frame; the weakened, wandering mind, so changed from what it used to be. And standing by that good Christian's bed, and thinking of the little child, I said to myself, There is the Beginning of life; Here is the End; — what shall we say in the view of that sad contrast? And I thought, there and then, that "Better is the end of a thing than the beginning!" Yes; better is the end of a dangerous voyage than its outset. You have seen a ship sailing away upon a long, perilous voyage over the ocean; the day was fair and sunshiny, and the ship looked gay and trim, with her white sails and her freshly-painted sides. And you have seen a ship coming safe into port at the end of her thousands of miles over the deep, under a gloomy, stormy sky, and with hull and masts battered by winds and waves. And you have thought, I dare say, that better far was this ending, safe and sure, than even that sunshiny beginning, with all the risks before it. And here, in the worn figure on the weary bed, here is the safe end of the voyage of life! Oh, what perils are yet before the merry little child! Who can say if that little one is to end in glory? But to the dying Christian all these perils are over. He is safe, safe! And then, remember, *this* is not yet the end, you see. It is NOT the end, that weary figure, lying on that bed of pain. It is only the last step before the end. A very little, and how glorious and happy that sufferer will be! You would not wish to keep him here, when you think of all the blessedness into which the next step from this pain will bear him. Nay; but you may take up, in a sublimer significance than that of deliverance from mere earthly ill, the beautiful words of the greatest poet :

> "Vex not his soul: oh, let him pass! He hates him,
> That would, upon the rack of this rough world,
> Stretch him out longer!"

CHAPTER IV.

GOING ON.

THERE are many things of which you have a much more vivid perception at some times than at others. The thing is before you; but sometimes you can grasp it firmly, sometimes it eludes you mistily. You are walking along a country path, just within hearing of distant bells. You hear them faintly; but all of a sudden, by some caprice of the wind, the sound is borne to you with startling clearness. There is something analogous to that in our perceptions and feelings of many great facts and truths. Commonly, we perceive them and feel them faintly; but sometimes they are borne in upon us, we cannot say how. Sometimes we get vivid glimpses of things which we had often talked of, but which we had never truly discerned and realized before. And for many days it has been so with me. I have seemed to feel the lapse of time with startling clearness. I have no doubt, my reader, that you have sometimes done the like. You have seemed to actually perceive the great current with which we are all gliding steadily away and away.

Rapid movement is a thing which has a certain power to disguise itself from the person who is involved in it. Every one knows that if you are travelling in an express train at sixty miles an hour, you do not feel the speed nearly so much as the man does who stands beside the track and sees the great mass sweep by like a hurricane. Have you ever thought it would be curious, if we could for a few minutes be made sensible of the world's motion?* Here we are, tearing on through space at an inconceivable speed. We do not feel it, of course; we could not stand it. I should like to feel it for half a minute — not for more.

But it is not *that* motion we are to think of at present. No special illumination has been accorded to me, making me feel that fact which we all know without feeling. But there is another rapid motion, common to all of us, as is the motion of the earth which bears us all. There is a great current bearing us along and all things about us, which is commonly not much felt. But it seems to me that for several weeks I have been actually feeling it. I have been excessively busy; living in a great pressure and hurry of occupations. In that state, my reader, you feel Sunday after Sunday return with a rapidity which takes away your breath; and let me say that if you have to provide one sermon, and still more if you have to provide two, against the return of each, you will in that fever of work and haste come to look from one Sunday to the next till you will come to find them flying past you like the quarter-mile posts on a railway. You will find that you can hardly believe, walking into church on Sunday morning, that a week has gone since the last Sunday. And in such a time you will realize much more distinctly than you usually do, that all things are going on, — drifting away, — all in company. These April days are taking life away from you, from me, — from prince and peasant. There is one thing at least which all human beings are using up at exactly the same rate. We can all get out of the day just twenty-four hours, neither more nor less. One man may live at the rate of a hundred pounds a year, and another at the rate of a hundred thousand; but each expends his time at the rate of three hundred and sixty-five days a year. Whatever other differences there may be between the lots of human beings, we are all drifting on with the current of time, and drifting at the same rate exactly. And we are certainly drifting. We are never quite the same in two successive weeks. One Sunday is not like the last. Look closely, and you will see that there is a difference, — slight perhaps, but real. Each time you sit down to your "Saturday Review" you feel there is a difference since the last time. Still more do you feel it, as you read the returning "Fraser," coming at the longer interval of a month. Things never come back again quite the same. And indeed in Nature there is a singular dislike to uniformity. If to-day be a fine day, look back; it is almost certain that this day last year was rainy. If to-day you are in very cheerful spirits, it is probable that on the corresponding day in the year that is gone you were very dull and anxious. No doubt human beings sometimes successfully resist Nature's love of variety. Some men have an especial love for having and doing things always in the same way. They walk on special days always on the same side of the street; perhaps they put their feet like Dr. Johnson, on the same stones in the pavement. They dress in the same way year after year. They maintain anniversaries, and try to bring the old party around the table once more, and to have the old time back. But we cannot have things exactly over again. There is a difference in the feeling, even if you are able precisely to reproduce the fact. And indeed the wonder is that things are so much like, as they are to-day, to what they were a year ago, when we think of the innumerable possibilities of change that hang over us. Yes, we are drifting on and on, down to the great sea. Sit down, my friend, to write your article. You have written many. The paper is the same; the table on which you write is the same; the inkstand is the same; and the pen is made by the same mender that made all the rest. And it is possible enough that when the article is printed at last, your readers will say that it is just the same thing over again; but it is not. To your feeling this day's work is quite different from the work of all preceding days. There is an undefinable variation from whatever was before. And as weeks and months go on, there come to be differences which some may think more real than any in the comparatively fanciful respect of feeling. The hair is turning thin and gray; the old spirit is subdued. There are changes in taste, in judgment, in feeling, in many ways. Yes, we are all Going On.

I wish to stop. There is something awful in this perpetual progression. If the current would slacken its speed, at least, and let one quietly think for a little while! Let us sit down, my friend, by the way-side. We are old enough now to look back, as well as to look round; and to think how life is going with us, and with those we know. We are now in the middle passage; perhaps farther on. And if we are half way in fact, assuredly we are far more in feeling. Though a man live to seventy, his first thirty-five years are by far the longer portion of his life.

Let us think to-day, my reader, of ourselves and of our friends; and of how it is faring with us as we go on.

It is a curious thing now, when we have settled to our stride, and are going on (in most cases) very much as we probably shall go on as long as we live, to compare what we are with what we promised at our entrance on life to be. You remember people who began with a tremendous flourish of trumpets,—people of whom there was a vague impression, more or less general, that they were to do great things. Sometimes this impression was confined to the man himself. Not unfrequently it was shared by his mother and his sisters. It occasionally extended to his father and his brothers. And in a few cases, generally in these cases not without some reason, it prevailed in the mind of his fellow-students. And it may be said, that a belief that some young lad is destined to do considerable things, if it be anything like universal among his college companions, must have some foundation. A belief to the same effect with regard to any young man, if confined to two or three of his intimate companions, is generally quite groundless; and if it exist only in the heart of his mother and of himself, it is quite sure to be absurd and idiotic. We can all, probably, remember individuals who, without any reason apparent to onlookers, cherished a most extraordinary high opinion of themselves; and one which was not at all taken down by frequently being beaten, and even distanced, in the competitions of College life. Such individuals, for the most part, indulged a very bitter and malicious spirit towards students more able and successful than themselves. I wish I could believe that modesty always goes with merit. I fear no rule can be laid down. I have beheld inordinate self-conceit in very clever fellows, as well as in very stupid ones. And I have beheld self-conceit developed in a degree which could hardly be exceeded, in individuals who were neither very clever nor very stupid, but remarkably ordinary in every way. Let me here remark, that I have known the most enthusiastic admiration excited in the breasts of one or two individuals by a very commonplace man. I mean admiration of his talents. And I beheld the spectacle with great wonder, not unmixed with indignation. I can quite understand man or woman feeling enthusi astic admiration for a great and wonderful genius. I can feel that warm admiration myself. And I can imagine its existing in youthful minds, even when the genius is dashed with great failings, or is of a very irregular nature. But the thing I wonder at, and cannot understand, is enthusiastic admiration professed and felt for dreary commonplace. I am not in the least surprised when I hear a young person, or indeed an old one, speaking in hyperbolical terms of the preaching of Bishop Wilberforce. I have heard it myself, and I know how brilliant and effective it is. But I really look with wonder at the young woman who professes equally enthusiastic admiration of the sermons of Dr. Log. I have heard Dr. Log preach. I could not for my life attend to his sermon. It was horribly tiresome. There was not in it a trace of pith or beauty. It approached to the nature of twaddle. I was awe-stricken when I heard it described in rapturous phrases. I recognized a superior intelligence. I. thought to myself, reversing Mr. Tickell's lines, "You hear a voice I cannot hear; you see a hand I cannot see." It is right to add, that the enthusiastic appreciators of Dr. Log were very few in number, and that they appeared to me nearly as stupid as Dr. Log himself.

But leaving Dr. Log and his admirers, let me say that very clever fellows, very stupid fellows, and very commonplace fellows, have started in life with a great flourish of trumpets. The vanity of many lads, leaving the University, is enormous. They expect to set the Thames on fire, to turn the world upside down. A few takings-down bring the best of them to modesty and sense. And the men for whom the flourish was loudest do sometimes, when all find their level, have to rest at a very low one. Many painful mortifications and struggles bring them to it. Oh! if talent and ambition could always be in a man, in just proportion! But I have known the most commonplace of men, with ambition that would have given enough to do to the abilities of Shakspeare. And we may perhaps say, that no one who begins with a great flourish ever fails to disappoint himself and his friends. He may do very well; he may do magnificently; but he does not come up to the great expectations formed of him. I was startled the other day to hear a certain man named as a failure, who has attained supreme eminence in his own walk in life, and that a conspicuous one. I said No; he is anything but a failure; he has attained extraordinary eminence; he is a great man. But the reply was, "Ah, we expected far more! We thought he would leave an impression on the age, and he has certainly not done that; while it seems certain he has done the best he is ever to do." But look round, my friend, and think how the world goes with those who set out with you. They are generally, I suppose, jogging on humbly and respectably. The present writer did not in his youth live among those from whom the famous of the earth are likely to be taken. One or two of the number have risen to no small eminence; but the lot of most has circumscribed their ambition. It is not in the Senate that he can look to find many of the names of his old companions. It is not likely that any will be buried in Westminster Abbey. The life of two or three may perhaps be written, if they leave behind them a warm friend who is not very busy. It does not matter. The nonsense has been taken out of us by the work of life. And on the whole, we are going creditably on.

It is worthy of notice, that things which at the beginning were very bad may be made good by a very small change wrought upon them. You see this in human beings, as they go on through life. You remember, I have no doubt, how various passages in the earlier writings of Mr. Tennyson, on which the "Quarterly Review" savagely fixed at their first publication, and which Mr. Tennyson's warmest admirers must admit to have been in truth very weak, affected and ridiculous, have by alterations of wonderfully small amount been brought to a state in which the most fastidious critic could find no fault in them

Just a touch from the master-hand did it all. You have in a homelier degree felt the same yourself, in correcting and re-writing your own crude and immature compositions. Often a very small matter takes away the mark of that Beast whose name shall not be mentioned here. I know a very distinguished preacher, really a pulpit orator, whose manner at his outset was remarkably awkward. No doubt he has devoted much pains to his manner since; though his art is high enough to conceal any trace of art. I heard him preach not long since; and his manner was singularly graceful; while yet there was no great change materially. You have remarked how the features of a girl's face, very plain at fourteen, have at twenty grown remarkably pretty. And yet the years have wrought no very great change. The face is unquestionably and quite recognizably the same; yet it has passed from plainness into beauty. And so, as we go on in life, you will find a man has got rid of some little intrusive folly which just makes the difference between his being very good and his being very bad. The man whose tendency to boast, or to exaggerate, or to talk thoughtlessly of others, made him appear a fool in his youth, has corrected that one evil tendency, and lo! he is quite altered — he is all right; he is a wise and good man. You would not have believed what a change for the better would be made by that little thing. You know, I dare say, how poor and bad are the first crude thoughts for your sermon or your article, thrown at random on the page. Yet when you have arranged and rounded them into a symmetrical, and accurate, and well-considered composition, it is wonderful how little change there is from the first rude sketch. Look at the waste scraps of paper before you throw them into the fire, and you will find some of your most careful and best sentences there, word for word. You have not been able to improve upon the way in which you first dashed them down.

There is a sad thing which we are all made to feel, as we are going on. It is, that we are growing out of things which we are sorry to outgrow. The firmest conviction that we are going on to what is better, cannot suppress some feeling of regret at the thought of what we are leaving behind. When I was a country parson, I used to feel very sorry to see a laurel or a yew growing out of the shape in which I remembered it; and which was associated with pleasant days. There was a dull pang at the sight. I remember well a little yew I planted with my own hand. It looks like yesterday since I held its top, while a certain man filled in the earth, and put the sod round its stem. For some time it appeared doubtful if that yew would live and grow; at last it was fairly established, and it began to grow vigorously the second year. For a year or two more, it was a neat, shaggy little thing; but then it began to put out tremendous shoots, and to grow out of my acquaintance. I felt I was losing an old friend. Many a time I had stood and looked at the little yew; I knew every branch of it; and always went to look at it when I had been a few days away. No doubt it was growing better; it was progressing with a yew's progress; I was getting a new friend better than the old one; yet I sighed for the old one that was gradually leaving me. You do not like to think that your little child must grow into something quite different from what it is now, must die into the grown up man or woman, must grow hardened to the world, and cease to be lovable as now. You would like to keep the little thing as it is, when it climbs on your knee, and lays a little soft cheek against your own. Even in the big girl of seven, that goes to school, you regret the wee child of three that you used to run after on the little green before your door; and in the dawn of cleverness and thought, though pleasant to see, still you feel there is something gone which you would have liked to keep. But it is an inevitable law, that you cannot have two inconsistent good things together. You cannot at once have your field green as it is in spring, and golden as it is in autumn. You cannot at once live in the little dwelling which was long your home, and which is surrounded by the memories of many years; and in the more beautiful and commodious mansion which your increasing wealth has been able to buy. You cannot at once be the merchant prince, wealthy, influential, esteemed by all, though gouty, ageing, and careworn; and the hopeful, light-hearted lad that came in from the country to push his way, and on whose early aspirations and struggles you look back with a confused feeling as though he were another being. You cannot at the same time be a country parson, leisurely and quiet, living among green fields and trees, and knowing the concerns of every soul in your parish; and have the privilege and the stimulus of preaching to a congregation of educated folk in town. Yet you would look round in silence and regret, when you look for the last time upon the scenes amid which you passed some considerable part of your life; even though you felt that the new place of your labors and your lot were ever so much better. And though you know it is well that your children should grow up into men and women, still you will sometimes be sorry that their happy childhood must pass so swiftly and so completely away; that it must be so entirely lost in that which is to come after it; that even in the healthy maturity of body and of mind there is so little that recalls to you the merry little boy or girl you used to know. Yes; we may have got on to something that is unquestionably better; but still we miss the dear old time and way. It is as with the emigrant, who has risen to wealth and position in the new world across the sea; but who often thinks, with fond regret, of the hills of his native land; and who, through all these years, has never forgotten the cottage where he drew his first breath, and the little church-yard where his father and mother are sleeping. Yes; you little man with the very curly hair, standing at that sofa turning over the leaves of a large Bible with pictures; stay as you are, as long as you can! For I may live to see you grow into something far less pleasant to see; but I shall never live to see you Lord Chancellor; though that distinguished post (it is well known) is the natural designation of a Scotch clergyman's son.

There is something rather awful implied in going on. Its possibilities are vast; you may yet have greatly to modify your opinion of any man who is still going on. The page is not finished yet; and it may be terribly blotted before it is done with. But the man who is no longer going on; the man who has finished his page and handed it in; is fixed and statuesque. There he is, forever. You may finally make up your mind about *him*. He can never do anything to disappoint you now. But very many men do live on, just to disappoint. They have done their best already; and they are going on producing work very inferior to what they once did, and to what we might expect of them. You go and hear a great preacher; not upon a special occasion, but in his own church, upon a common Sunday. You have read his published sermons, and thought them very fine; some sentences from them still linger on your ear. Unhappily, he did not stop with these fine things. He is going on still; and what he is turning off now is quite different. There is little to remind you of what he was. Your lofty idea of that great and good man is sadly shattered. No doubt this is not always so. There are men who go on through life; and go on without deterioration. There are men who are always themselves; always up to the mark. But for the most part, going on implies a great falling off. Think of Sir Walter Scott's last novels. Think of Byron's last poetry. Compare "The Virgin Widow" with "Philip Van Artevelde" Think of the latter productions of the author of "Festus." Think of the last squeezings from the mind of Dr. Chalmers. Think of the recent appearances, intellectual and moral, of Mr. Walter Savage Landor. Think how roaring Irish patriots have become the pensioners of the Saxon, after having publicly sworn never to touch the alien coin. Think how men who bearded the tyrant in their youth, have ended in contented toadyism. We are never perfectly safe in forming a judgment of any man who is still going on; that is, of any living man. We shall not call him good, any more than happy, till we have seen the last of him. His very ending may be enough to blight all his past life. You cannot as yet settle the mark of a man who is still painting pictures, still publishing poems, still writing books, still speaking in parliament, still taking a prominent part in public business. He may possibly rise far above anything he has yet done. He may possibly sink so far below it, as to lower the general average of his entire life. As regards fame, the right thing is an end like Nelson's.* *He* ended at his best; and ended definitively. Even Trafalgar would have been over-clouded if the hero had still kept going on. Think of him perhaps coming back; being made a Duke; evincing great vanity; trying to become a leader among the Peers, and showing his lack of business aptitude and of sound judgment in politics; coming to be occasionally hissed about the streets of London getting involved in discreditable tricks to gain office. Now Nelson might have done none of these things. But I believe any one who reads his life will feel that he might have done them all. And was it not far better that the weak, but great man, the true hero, the warm-hearted, lovable, brave, honest admiral, should be taken away from the petty and sordid possibilities of Going On; that it should be made sure he should never vex or disappoint us; that he should die in a blaze of glory, and leave a name for every Briton to cherish and to love? There are living men, concerning whom we might regret that they are still going on. They cannot rise above their present estimation; they may well sink below it. It would be a great thing if some means could be devised, by which a man might stop, without dying. A man might say, after having done some difficult and honorable work, reaching over a large portion of his life, "Now, I stop here. I take my stand on what I have done; judge of me by that. I must still go on breathing the air as before; but I fear I shall let myself down; so don't inquire about me any further.' We all know that great and good men have sometimes, in the latter chapters of their life, done things on which we can but shut our eyes, and which we can but strive to forget. It seems quite certain that Solomon, albeit the wisest of men, became a weak old fool in his latter days; nor does the only reliable history say anything of final repentance and amendment. And silly or evil doings early in life, may be effaced from remembrance by wise and good doings afterwards; while silly and evil doings in the last stage of life, appear to stamp the character of it all.

It is this thought which sometimes makes the recollection that we are still going on, weigh heavily on one. There is no saying how the page of our life may be blotted before it is finished; and you must let me say, my friend, that the wise man will stand in great fear and suspicion of himself; and will very earnestly apply for that sacred influence which alone can hold him right to the end, where alone it is to be found. There are many things to make one thoughtful, as we remember how we are going on; but the great thing (as regards one's self) is, after all, the sight of the gloom before us, into which we are advancing day by day; not seeing even a step ahead. And to *that* may be added the occasional examples which are pressed upon us in the case of others, who once seemed very much like ourselves, of what human beings may come to be. And that which man has done, man may do. I see various things that are worthy of note, as I look round on the procession of the human beings I know and remember, and think what comes as we go on. I see some who are rather battered and travel-stained. The greatness of the way is beginning to tell. I see some who look somewhat worn and jaded. There are little physical symptoms of the wear of the machine. The hair of certain men is going, or even gone. The teeth of some are not complete, as of yore. On the whole, I trust, we are gaining. I do not think there is any period of life that one would wish to live over again; no period, at least, of more than a very few days. There are wrecks, no doubt; some who broke down early, and have quite disappeared, one does not know where; and among these, more than one or two whose promise was of the best.

Thinking of this one day, I was walking along a certain street, and came to a place where it was needful to cross. A carriage stopped the way, if that indeed can be called a carriage which was no more than a cab. And my attention was attracted by the cab-horse, which was standing close by the pavement. He was a sorry creature; but, as you looked at him, there was no mistaking the thoroughbred. There was the light head, once so graceful; the dilated, sensitive nostrils were still there, and the slender legs. But the poor legs were bent and shaky; the neck was cut into by the collar; the hair was rubbed off the skin in many places; and the sides were going with that peculiar motion which indicates broken wind. Here was what the poor horse had come to. At first doubtless he was a graceful, cheerful creature, petted and made much of in his youth. Probably he proved not worth training for a race-horse; and a thoroughbred without sufficient bone and muscle is very useless for practical purposes; though it may be remarked that a thoroughbred with sufficient bone and muscle is the best horse for every kind of work except drawing coals or beer. So the poor thing became a riding-hack, and having fallen a few times, was sold for a cab-horse. And it was plain that for many days he had been poorly fed, and hardly worked; and that now the cab-proprietor was taking all he could out of him, before giving him over to the knacker, to be made into sausages. It is a popular delusion that the last stage in a horse's existence is to go to the dogs. There are some districts in which he goes to the pigs; and others in which he ends by affording nutriment, in a disguised form, to human beings. I am no alarmist, and I believe horse-flesh is quite salutary. All I have to add is, that persons having an antipathy to that article of food, had better inquire where their bacon was fed, and had better keep a sharp eye upon their sausages.

This, however, is a digression from a sad reflection.

That poor cab-horse suggested various human beings whom I once knew. We have all known clever and promising youths who became drunken wrecks, and who deviated into various paths of sin, shame, and ruin. I laid down my pen when I had written that sentence, and thought of four, five, six, who had ended so, thinking of them not without a tear. Some were the very last you would have expected to come to this. There are indeed men whose career as youths is quite of a piece with their after-career of shame; but my early friends were not such as these. I can think of some, cheerful, amiable, facile in the hand of companions good or bad, who bade fair for goodness and happiness, yet who went astray, and who were wrecked very soon. I knew of one, once a man of high character and good standing, who had to become as one dead, and who was long afterwards traced, a sailor in distant seas. He had a beautiful voice; and I have heard that it was fine to hear him singing on the deck by moonlight as he kept his watch. Poor wretch, with what a heavy heart!

The change that passes upon one's self, as we go on through life, comes so gradually through the wear of successive days, that we are hardly conscious how perceptibly we are getting through all that we have to get through here. We fancy, quite honestly, that we do not look any older in the last ten years, and that we are now just the same as we were ten years since.

We fancy that, intellectually and morally, we are better; and physically, just the same. People whose character and history are commonplace at least fancy this in their more cheerful hours. But sometimes it comes home to us what a change has passed on us, perhaps in not a very long time. You will feel this especially in reading old letters and diaries; the letters you wrote and the diary you kept long ago. You probably thought that your present handwriting is exactly the same as your handwriting of ten years since; but when you put the two side by side, you will see how different they are. And in the perusal of these ancient documents, it will be borne in upon you how completely changed are the things you care for. The cares and interests, the fears and hopes, of the old days, are mainly gone. You have arrived at quite different estimates of people and of things; and if you be a wiser, you are doubtless a sadder man. And when you go back to the school-boy spot, or to the house where you lived when you were ten years old, it will be a curious thing to contrast the little fellow of that time, with your own grave and sobered self. And you will do so the more vividly in the presence of some well-remembered object, which has hardly changed at all in the years which have changed you so much. It is a commonplace; but commend me to commonplaces for reaching the common heart; the picture of the aged man, or even the man in middle age, standing beside the tree or the river by which he played when he was a little child. The hills, the fields, the trees around, are the same; and there is he, so changed! You remember Wordsworth's beautiful ballad, in which the old schoolmaster is lying beside the fountain, by which he was used to lie in his days of youthful strength; you remember the same old man, looking back, from a bright April morning, to another April morning exactly like it, but past for forty years. We may well believe, that there is not a human being but knows the feeling. It is some little thing in our own history that we remember; but it has touched the electric chain of association, and wakened up the past. There is a rude song current among the coal-miners of the north of England, in which an old man is standing by an old oak-tree, and speaking to that unchanged friend of the change that has passed upon himself; and though the chorus, recurring at the end of each verse, is not so graceful as the lines which Wordsworth gives to Matthew, the thought is exactly the same. The words are, "Sair failed, hinny, sair failed now; sair failed, hinny, sin I kenned thou." But of all the poems which contrast the much-changed man and the little-changed tree, I know of none more touching than one I lately read in an American magazine. It is called "The Name in the Bark." Here is a part of the poem: —

> The self of so long ago,
> And the self I struggle to know,
> I sometimes think we are two, — or are we shadows of one?

To-day the shadow I am,
Comes back in the sweet summer calm,
To trace where the earlier shadow flitted awhile in the sun.

Once more in the dewy morn,
I trod through the whispering corn:
Cool to my fevered cheek soft breezy kisses were blown:
The ribboned and tasselled grass
Leaned over the flattering glass;
And the sunny waters trilled the same low musical tone.

To the gray old birch I came,
Where I whittled my schoolboy name:
The nimble squirrel once more ran skippingly over the rail:
The blackbirds down among
The alders noisily sung,
And under the blackberry-trees whistled the serious quail.

I came, remembering well,
How my little shadow fell,
As I painfully reached and wrote to leave to the future a sign:
There, stooping a little, I found
A half-healed, curious wound; —
An ancient scar in the bark, but no initial of mine!

I shall not add the verses in which the poet wisely moralizes on this instance how fast the traces we leave behind us pass away. Is it because I can remember how *my* little shadow fell, many years since, that the last-quoted verse touches me as it does? We cast a different shadow now, my friend, from that little one we remember well; and it will not be very long till the shadows that fell and the substance that cast them shall have left here an equal trace.

Yes, my readers, we are all changed, as we are going on, from what we used to be. And it is no wonder we are changed. The wonder is that we are not changed a great deal more. How much hard work we have done; how much care, trouble, anxiety, disappointment, we have come through! What painful lessons we have been obliged to learn, every one of us! A great deal of the work we do is merely to serve the purposes of the time, and it leaves no trace; but when the work done leaves its tangible memorial, it often strikes us much; and we wonder to see how fresh and unwearied the man looks who did it all. I have seen the accumulated stock of sermons of a clergyman of more than forty years in the Church. It was awful to see what a vast mass they were. And even when we look not at the work of a lifetime, but at the results of what was no more than part of the work of a few years, we do so with a feeling of surprise that the man who did it was not at the end of his work much changed to appearance from what he was when he began it. Some time since I got back for a short time the prize essays I wrote while at college. They filled a whole shelf, and not a very small shelf. It was awful to look at them. They were all written before the writer was twenty-two. They were great heavy volumes — heavy physically; and intellectually and æsthetically still heavier. I tried to read one, but could not, because it was so tiresome; and I may therefore fairly conclude that no one will ever read them. Yet let me confess, that having arranged them on a lower shelf, I sat down on a rocking-chair immediately in front of them, and looked at them with great interest and wonder. In such a prospect, what could one do but shake one's head and sigh? The essays were all successful, Mr. Snarling. Every one of those prize essays got its prize. It is not in mortification that one sighs, but vaguely in the view of such an immense deal of hard work done to so very small purpose. And when you look at a man advanced in life, whose whole life has been one of hard work, you cannot but confusedly wonder to see him looking as he does. To see Lord Campbell walking about at Hartrigge, when he had reached the highest place that a British subject can reach, — to see the benignant and cheerful face of that remarkable man, and then to think of the tremendous amount of mental labor he had gone through in his long life, was a most perplexing and bewildering sight. When you are shown a ship that has come back from an Arctic voyage, you will generally remark that the ship looks like it; it has a weather-beaten and battered aspect, suggestive of crunching against icebergs and the like. But when you are shown a man whose voyage in life has been a long and laborious one, you are sometimes surprised to find that he looks as fresh and unwearied as if he had done nothing all his life but amuse himself.

I have already said that it is a great blessing that in this world there are such things as *Beginnings and Ends.* It is a blessing that we can divide our way, as we go on, into stages, — that we are saved the wearying and depressing effect of a very long uniform look-out. We begin a succession of tasks; we end them; — and then we begin afresh. And even those things in which, in fact, there are no beginnings nor ends, have them in our feeling. The unvarying advance of time is broken into days and weeks; and we feel a most decided end on Saturday night, and we make a new start on Monday morning. It must be dreadful for a man to work straight on, Sunday and all other days. I believe it is impossible that any man should do so long. The man who refuses to observe a weekly day of rest will knock his head against the whole system of things, to the detriment of his head.

But even more valuable than this obvious result of the existence of Beginnings and Ends is another. It is an unspeakable blessing that a man who has got himself thoroughly into a mess anywhere or in any occupation, should be able to get away somewhere else and begin again. If Mr. Snarling, who has quarrelled with all his parishioners in his present charge, were removed to another a hundred miles off, I think he would take great pains to avoid those acts of folly and ill-temper which have made him so unhappy where he is. And let me say in addition, that most of us, as we go on, are always in our hearts admitting the imperfection and unsatisfactoriness of our past life. We are every now and then, in thought and feeling, beginning again. Men are every now and then cutting off the past; and acknowledging that they must start, or (more commonly) that a little while back they *did* start, anew. You occasionally avow to yourself, my reader, though not to the world, that you were a blockhead even two or three years ago. You occasionally say to yourself that your real life begins from this day three years. From that date you think you have been a great deal wiser and better. That course of conduct five years ago; those opinions you held then, that poem, essay, or book you wrote then; you are willing to give up. You have not a word to say for them. But *that* was in a former stage — in a different life. You have begun again since that; you have cut connection with it. You say to yourself, "It may be thirty years since I came into the world; but my real life — the part of my life I am willing to avow and to answer for — began on the 1st of January, 1860. I cut off all that preceded. I began again then; and as for what I have said and done since then, I am ready (as Scotch folk say) to *stand on the head of it.* It is only in a limited sense that I admit my identity with the individual who before that date bore my name and wore my aspect. I disavow the individual. I condemn him as severely as you can do." Tell me, my reader, have you not many a time done that? Have you not given up one leaf as hopelessly blotted, and tried to turn over a new one, — cut off (in short) the preceding days of life and resolved to begin again? Do so, my friend. You may make something of the new leaf, but you will never make anything of the old one. And whenever you find any human being anxious to begin again, always let him do it, always help him to do it. Don't do as some malicious wretches do, try to make it as difficult and humiliating as possible for him to turn over the new leaf. Don't try to compel him to a formal declaration in words that he sees his former life was wrong, and wants to break away from it; it was bitter enough for him to make that avowal to himself. You will find malicious animals who, if man or child has done wrong, and is sorry for it, and wishes to turn into a better way, will do all they can to prevent the poor creature from quietly turning away from the blurred page and beginning the clean one. If there be joy in heaven over the repenting sinner, it cannot be denied that there is vicious spite over the repenting sinner in certain hearts upon earth. Let us not seek to make repentance harder than it is by its nature. Unhappily there are cases in which neither in fact nor in feeling is it possible to begin again, — at least upon an unsullied page. There are many people who never have a second chance. They must go deeper and deeper; they took the wrong turning, and they can never go back. Such is generally the result of crime.

There is one sex, at least, with which the one wrong step is irretraceable. And even with the ruder half of mankind, there are some deeds which, being done shut you in like the spring-lock in poor Ginevra's oak-chest. There is no repassing; and often the irreversible turning into the wrong track was not the result of anything like crime; often the cause was no more than ill-luck, or some foolish word or doing. What disproportionate punishment often follows on little acts of haste or folly! In the order of Providence folly is often punished much more severely than sin. A young fellow, foolishly thinking to gain the favor of a sporting patron by exhibiting an extraordinary knowledge of the turf and the chase, cuts himself off from the living on which his heart was set. A flippant word, hardly spoken till it was repented, has prejudicially affected a man's whole after-career. Various men, in pique and haste, have made marriages which blighted all their life, and which brought an actual sorer punishment than that with which the law visits aggravated burglary or manslaughter. It is well in most cases to keep a way of retreat. It is well that before entering in you should see if you can get out, should it prove desirable. You must be very confident or very desperate if you cut off the bridge behind you, when in front there is but to do or to die. No doubt a habit of keeping the retreat open is fatal to decision of action and character. There is good, in one view, in feeling that we have crossed the Rubi con and are *in for it*; then we shall hold stoutly on; otherwise, we may be advancing with only half a heart. And there are important cases in which the difference between half a heart and a whole one makes just the difference between signal defeat and splendid victory.

It is to be admitted, my friends, that as we go on, the nonsense is being taken out of us. You have seen a horse start upon its journey in a very frisky condition, kicking about and prancing; but after a few miles it settles into doing its work steadily. That is the image which to my mind represents our career, going on. The romance has mainly departed. We look for homely things, and are content with them. Once, too, we expected to do great achievements, but not now. We know, generally, our humble mark. Indeed, the question as to the earning of bread and butter has utterly crowded out of our hearts the question as to the attainment of fame. We would not give one pound six and eight pence for wide renown. We would not give the eight pence for posthumous celebrity. We know our humble mark, I have said. I mean intellectually. And it is a great comfort to know it. It saves us much fever of competition, of suspense, of disappointment. We cannot possibly be beaten in the race of ambition; we cannot even injure our lungs or our heart in the race of ambition; because we shall not run it at all. A wise man may be very glad, and very thankful, that he does not think himself a great genius, and that he does not think what he can do very splendid. For if a man thought himself a great genius, he would be bitterly mortified that he was not recognized as such. And if a man thought his sermons or his books very fine, he would be mortified that his church was not crammed to suffocation, instead of being quite pleased when it is respectably filled; and he would be disappointed that his books do not sell by scores of thousands of copies, instead of being joyful that about half the first edition sells, leaving his publishers or himself only a little out of pocket, besides all their time and trouble. I know a man of highly respectable talents, who once published a theological book. Nobody ever bought a copy except himself. But he bought a good many, which he gave to his friends. And then he was extremely pleased that so many copies were sold. Was he not a wise and modest man?

Among other follies, I think that in going on, men, if they have any sense at all, get rid of Affectation. Few middle-aged men, unless they be by nature incurably silly and conceited, try to walk along the street in a dignified and effective way. They wish to get quickly and quietly along; and they have utterly discarded the idea that any passer-by thinks it worth while to look at them. Generally speaking, they sign their names in a natural handwriting. They do not, as a rule, look very cheerful. They seem, when silent, to fall into calculations, the result of which is not satisfactory. The great tamer of men, is doubtless, the want of money. *That* is the thing that brings people down from their airy flights and romantic imaginations; especially when there are some dependent on them. You may dismiss the very rich, who never need think and scheme about money, and how it is to be got, and how far it can be made to go, as an inappreciable fraction of the human race. Care sits heavy upon the great majority of those who are going on. You know the anxious look, and the inelastic step, of most middle-aged people who have children. All these things are the result of the want of money. Probably the want of money serves great ends in the economy of things. Probably it is a needful and essential spur to work; and a useful teacher of modesty, humility, moderation. No man will be blown up with a sense of his own consequence, or walk about fancying that he is being pointed out with the finger as the illustrious Smith, when (like poor Leigh Hunt) he fears lest the baker should refuse to send him bread, or that the washerwoman should impound his shirts. It is a lamentable story that is set out in the latter portions of the "Correspondence" of that amiable but unwise man. And human vanity needs a strong pressure to keep it within moderate limits. Even the wise man, with all his unsparing efforts to keep self-conceit down, has latent in him more of it than he would like to confess. I lately heard of an outburst of the vanity latent in a decent farmer of moderate means. One market day he got somewhat drunk, unhappily. And walking home, on the country road, he fell into a ditch, wherein he remained. Some of his friends found him there, and proceeded to rescue him. On approaching him, they found he was praying. For though drunk that day, he was really a worthy man: it was quite an exceptional case; I suppose he never got drunk again. They caught a sentence of his prayer. It was, "*Lord, as Thou hast made me great so do Thou make me good!*" His friends had no idea of the high estimation in which the man held himself. He was, in the matter of greatness, exactly on the same footing with the other people round him. But he did not think so. In his secret soul, he fancied himself a very superior man. And when his self-restraint was removed by whiskey, the fancy came out.

But he must have been at least a well-to-do man, who had this idea of his own importance. Many men are burdened far too heavily for that. Very many men in this world are bearing just as much as they can. A little more would break them down, as the last pound breaks the camel's back. When a man is loaded with as much work, or suffering, or disappointment, as he can bear, a very trifling addition will make his burden greater than he can bear. I remember how a friend told me of a time when he was passing through the greatest trouble of his life. He had met a very heavy trial, but was bearing up wonderfully. One day, only a day or two after the stroke had fallen, he was walking along a lonely and rocky path, when he tripped and fell down, giving his knee a severe stunning blow against a rock. He had been able to bear up before, though his heart was full. But that was the drop too much; and he broke down and cried like a child, though before *that* he had not shed a tear.

There are various conclusions at which men arrive as they go on, which at an earlier part of their journey they would have rejected with indignation. One thing you will learn, my reader, as you advance, is, what you may expect. I mean, in particular, how much you may expect from the kindness of your friends; how much they are likely to do for you; how much they are likely to put themselves about to serve you. I do not say it in the way of finding fault; but the ordinary men of this world are so completely occupied in looking to their own concerns, that they have no time or strength to spare for those of others. And, accordingly, if you stick in the mud, you had much better, in all ordinary cases, try to get out yourself. Nobody is likely to help you particularly. Good Samaritans, in modern society, are rare; priests and levites are frequent. I lately came to know a man who had faithfully and effectually served a certain cause for many years. He came at last to a point in his life at which those interested in the cause he had served might have greatly helped him. He made sure they would. But they simply did nothing. Nobody moved a finger to aid that meritorious man. He was mortified; but after waiting a little, he proceeded to help himself, which he did effectually. I do not think he will trust to his friends any more. The truth is, that beyond the closest circle of relationship, men in general care very little indeed for each other. I know men, indeed, — and I say it with pride and thankfulness, — with whom the case is very different: I remember one who loved his friends as himself, and who stood up for them everywhere with a noble devotion. I think a good many of them caught from him the impulse that would have made them do as much for *him;* but *he* was one of the truest friends and the noblest-hearted men on this earth. Many months are gone since he was laid in his grave; but how many of those who will read this page cherish more warmly than ever the memory of John Parker! "If I forget thee," my beloved friend — you remember David's solemn words. But compared with the chance acquaintances whom every one knows, *he* was as a Man among Gorillas. And I recur to my principle, that beyond closest ties of blood, men in general care very little for one another. You have known, I dare say, an old gentleman, dying in great suffering through many weeks; but his old club friends did not care at all; at most, very little. His suffering and death caused them not the slightest appreciable concern. You may expect certain of your friends to be extremely lively and amusing at a dinner-party, on the day of your funeral. I remember, a good many years ago, feeling very indignant at learning about a gay entertainment, where was much music and dancing, attended by a number of young people, on the evening of the day on which a fair young companion of them all was laid in her last resting-place. I am so many years older; yet I confess I have not succeeded in schooling myself to feel none of the indignation I then felt; though I have thoroughly got rid of the slightest tendency to the surprise I felt in that inexperienced time. For, since then, I have seen a young fellow of six-and-twenty engaged in a lively flirtation with two girls who were in a railway carriage while he was standing on the platform, just the day after his mother's funeral. I have beheld two young ladies decked to go out to a ball. Their dresses happily combined a most becoming aspect with the expression of a modified degree of mourning. They had recently lost a relative. The relative was their father. I have witnessed the gayety and the flirtations of a newly-made widow. It appeared to me a sorry sight. There are human beings, it cannot be denied, whose main characteristics are selfishness and heartlessness. For it is unquestionably true, that the most thorough disregard for the feelings, and wishes, and interests of others, may coexist with the keenest concern for one's self.

You will find people who bear with a heroic constancy the sufferings and trials of others; but who make a frightful howling about their own. And, singularly, those who never gave sympathy to another mortal, expect that other mortals shall evince lively sympathy with them. Commend me to a thoroughly selfish person, for loud complaints of the selfishness of others.

As you go on, you will come to understand how well you can be spared from this world. You remember Napoleon's axiom, that No man is necessary. There is no man in the world whom the world could not do without. There are many men who, if they were taken away, would be missed; would be very much missed, perhaps, by more or fewer human beings. But there is no man but what we may say of him that, useful and valuable as he may be, we might, sooner or later, with more or less difficulty, come to do without him. The country got over the loss of Sir Robert Peel and the Duke of Wellington; it misses Prince Albert yet, but it is getting over his absence. I do not mean to say that there are not hearts in which a worthy human being is always remembered, and always missed; in which his absence is felt as an irreparable loss, making all life different from what it used to be. But in the case of each, these hearts are few. And it is quite fit that they should be few. If our sympathy with others were as keen as our feeling for ourselves, we should get poorly through life; with many persons sympathy is only too keen and real as it is. But though you quite easily see and admit that human beings can be spared without much inconvenience, when you think how the State comes to do without its lost political chief, and the country without its departed hero, you are somewhat apt, till growing years have taught you, to cherish some lurking belief that you yourself will be missed, and kindly remembered, longer and by more people than you are ever likely to be. A great many clergymen, seeing the strong marks of grief evinced by their congregation as they preach their farewell sermon before going to another parish, can hardly think how quickly the congregation will get over its loss; and how soon it will come to assemble Sunday by Sunday with no remembrance at all of the familiar face that used to look at it from the pulpit, or of the voice which once was pleasant to hear. Let no man wilfully withdraw from his place in life, thinking that he will be missed so much that he will be eagerly sought again. If you step out of the ranks, the crowd may pass on; the vacant space may be occupied; and you may never be able to find your place any more. There are far more men than there are holes, and all the holes get filled up. Who hastily resigned a bishopric? who in dudgeon threw up an Attorney-Generalship? who (thinking he could not be spared) abdicated the Chancellorship? And did not each of these men find out his mistake? The holes were filled up, and the men remained outsiders ever afterwards. There is a very striking story of Hawthorne's, analyzing the motives and feelings of a man who, in some whim, went away from his house and his wife, but went no farther than the next street, and lived there in disguise for many years, all his relatives fancying him dead. And the eminent American shows, with wonderful power, how a human being so acting may make himself the outlaw of the universe. It needs all your presence, all your energy, all your present services, to hold you in your place in life, my friend. There are certain things whose value is felt through their absence; but I think that, as a general rule, a man can make his value felt only by his presence.

A friend of mine, who is a successful author, told me how, when he published his first book, he made quite sure that all his friends would read it, and more particularly that all his cousins, to whom he sent copies of his book, would do so. But he confided to me, as one of the lessons he had arrived at in going on, that it is with total strangers that any writer must hope for whatever success he may reach. Your cousins, thinking to mortify you, will diligently refrain from reading your volume. At least they will profess that they do so; though you will find them extremely well coached up in all the weak and foolish passages with which the reviewers have found fault. And these passages they will hasten to point out to your father and mother, also to your wife, at the same time expressing their anxious hope that these foolish passages may not do you harm. My friend told me how in his first book there was a sentence which his cousins feared would give offence to a certain eminent person who had shown him kindness; and the promptitude with which they could always turn up the passage, and the vigorous and fluent manner in which they could point out how offensive it must prove to the eminent person, testified to the amount of pains they had bestowed upon the discussion of the subject. Among the six hundred pages, how easily and swiftly they could always find this unlucky page! My friend told me that in a rather popular book of his, there was a passage of a few pages in length which had been severely criticised. Possibly it was weak; possibly it was absurd. I confess that I read it, and it did not strike me as remarkable. However, the critics generally attacked it; and probably they were right. A few weeks ago, my friend told me he met a very pretty young cousin, of twenty years, for the first time. With a radiant smile, the fair cousin began to talk to my friend about his efforts in authorship. "Oh, Mr. Smith," said she, "do you know, the only thing I ever read in your book was that part where you said" — no matter what. "It was so funny! Do you know, Cousin Dick showed it to me the moment I arrived at Ananias Street!" I have not the faintest doubt that Cousin Dick did. I have myself heard Dick quote a sentence from his relative's work, which sounded very flippant and presumptuous. I turned up the page, and requested Dick to observe that he was (unintentionally, but) grossly misrepresenting the passage. It was not the least like what he quoted; and the version given by him was altered greatly for the worse. Dick saw he was wrong. But several times since have I heard him give the incorrect quotation, just as before. Of course, his purpose was not to represent his relative as a man of taste and sense.

I think that as we go on we come to have a great charity for the misdoings of our fellow-men. There are, indeed, flagrant crimes, whose authors can never be thought of but with a burning abhorrence. I have heard of the doings of men whom I should be happy to help to hang. But I am thinking of the little misdoings of social life in a civilized country. As for deliberate cruelty and oppression, as for lying and cheating to make money, I never have learned to think of them but with a bitterness approaching the ferocious. Nor have I grown a bit more charitable with advancing years in my estimate of the liar, cheat, and blackguard (of whatever rank), who will mislead some poor girl to her ruin. I should be glad to burn such a one, with this hand, with a red-hot iron, upon the forehead, with the word LIAR. And something of the emotion I feel in the thought of him extends to the thought of the young ladies who waltz with him, knowing perfectly what he is; and to the thought of the parsons who toady him, in hope of a presentation to the wealthy living of Soapy-cum-Sneaky. But, setting these extreme cases aside, you will come, as you go on through life, to see some excuse for various little misdoings, towards which you felt somewhat bitterly in earlier years. You will come to frankly recognize the truth, which at first you are slow to admit, that there are certain positions which are too much for human nature. I mean too much for human nature to hold without exhibiting a good deal of pettiness, envy, spitefulness, and malevolence; unless, indeed, with very fine and amiable natures. There is an ecclesiasiastical arrangement peculiar to Scotland; it is what is termed a *Collegiate Charge*. It means that a parish church shall have two incumbents of authority, dignity, and eminence, exactly similar. The incumbents, in many cases, quarrel outright; in many more they do not work cordially together. In a smaller number, indeed, they have been known to be as brothers, or as father and son. There is something trying in the position of a parish clergyman who has a curate, or assistant, who is more popular than himself. You may sometimes find a church poorly attended when the clergyman preaches, but crowded when the curate does so. Even in such a case, if the rector be a good man, and the curate another, perfect kindliness may exist between the rector and the curate; but I doubt whether that kindliness is much to be expected from the rector's wife. And when the curate at length gets a parish of his own, he need not expect that his old principal will often ask him back to preach. Now, many people will be found ready to speak with much severity of the principal who acts thus; and to blame the clergyman who, not being able to fill his church himself, prefers having it empty to seeing it filled by any one else. Such people are unquestionably wrong. They expect from the poor clergyman more than ought to be looked for from average human nature. The clergyman's conduct is very natural. Put yourself in his place; look at the matter from his point of view. You would not like yourself the thing he does not like. You would very possibly do exactly what he does. And you might do it all quite conscientiously. You might fancy you had high and pure reasons for what you did, and that there was no intrusion of jealousy. The young curate's sermons were, very likely, very crude and extravagant; and you may honestly think it your duty to prevent your people from being presented with spiritual food so immature. And rely upon it, those men who carefully exclude from their pulpits all intresting and attractive preachers, and put there (in their own absence) the dullest and poorest preachers they can find, though doubtless actuated in great measure by a determination that they themselves shall not be eclipsed, but shall rather shine by comparison, are quite able to persuade themselves that they act from the purest motives. But even while you pity the men (let us hope there are very few) in whose mind such unworthy considerations have weight, do not blame them severely. They are in a difficult position. No doubt they would find it happier as well as worthier to spurn the first suggestion of petty jealousy; no doubt the magnanimous man would do so; but there are men who are not magnanimous, and who could no more be magnanimous than they could be six feet high, or than they could write *King Lear*. Now, my friend, as you go on, you come to understand all these things. You learn to make great allowances for the pettiness of human nature. You come to be able to treat with cordiality people to whom in your hot and hasty youth you could not have spoken without giving them a bit of your mind which they would not have liked to hear. And when I say that with advancing years you come to excuse human misdoings, I do not mean that as we grow older we come to think more lightly of the difference between right and wrong, or between the generous and the mean. I hope we know better than that. It is another principle that comes into play — the principle, to wit, that not being without sin yourself, you should be slow to cast a stone at an erring brother. It has been already said that there are cases as to which we shall not reason thus. Of heartless and deliberate cruelty and treachery we shall never think but with fury; and we do not wish ever to think but with fury. Give me the knout, and lead out one of several human beings of whom I have heard, and I will warrant you you should hear extensive howling! I am not afraid to plead the highest of all precedents, for the permission of the bitterest wrath and for the dealing of the sharpest blows. But I humbly and firmly trust, my friendly reader, that in you and me there is nothing like heartless, deliberate cruelty and treachery. We have no sympathy at all with these, any more than with the peculiar taste which makes worms like filth. But as to very much of human error and weakness, do you not feel in yourself the capacities which (though restrained by God's grace) might have brought you to all that? The thing we can least forgive is that which we cannot imagine how any one could do — that which we think we have in us nothing like.

In your earlier days, you were perpetually getting into scrapes, by speaking hastily and acting hastily. As you go on, you learn by experience to avoid these things in great measure; and you learn to be very cautious as to the people you will take into your confidence. It is a sorrowful lesson of experience, but it *is* a lesson of experience, that there are many people to whom you should never say a sentence, without first calculating whether that sentence can be repeated, or can be misrepresented, to your disadvantage. Like a skilful chess-player, you need to consider what may be the result of this move. It is to be admitted, that much of worldly wisdom is far from being a pleasing or noble thing. You learn by experience a great deal which it is right you should know and act upon, yet which does not ennoble you. It is a fine sight, after all, a warm-hearted, outspoken, injudicious man of more than middle age! I know well an eminent professor in a certain university, who is a very clever and learned man, and a very injudicious one. I admire his talents and his learning; but I feel a warm affection for his outspoken and injudicious honesty and truthfulness. I am quite sure that if he thought a neighboring marquis a humbug, he would call him one. I have the strongest ground for believing that if he thought a bishop a fool, he would say so. Let us ever try to hold our prudence free from the suspicion of baseness. I trust that as we go on, we are not coming to practise sneaky arts to the end of getting on. Sneakiness, and underhand dealing, are doubtless to be reckoned among the arts of self-advancement. Honesty is, in many cases, unquestionably the very worst policy. But though honesty be so, honesty is the right thing, after all! But honest men sometimes think to possess, together, two inconsistent things. They think to possess the high sense of scrupulous integrity; and at the same time the favor, patronage, and profit, which can be had only by parting with *that.*

We are all going on: a man here and there is also getting on. As you look round upon the people who started with you, you will discern that even those who are doing well in life, for the most part reached their utmost elevation before very many years were gone; and for a large tract of time past have not been gaining. They are going on, in short: Time makes sure that we all shall do *that;* but they are not getting on. Their income is just the same now that it was five or ten years since; and the estimation in which they are held by those who know them has neither grown nor lessened. But there is a man here and there who is growing bigger as well as growing older. He is coming, yearly, to be better known; he is gaining in wealth, in influence, in reputation. Every walk of life has its rising men. There are country gentlemen who gradually elbow their way forward among the members of their class, till they stand conspicuously apart from them. So with painters, authors, barristers, preachers. Who are they, among those whom I know, who are making way, and rising in the world? And what is the secret of their success? I must stop and think.

CHAPTER V.

CONCERNING DISAGREEABLE PEOPLE.

ON the whole, it was very disagreeable.

Thus wrote a certain great traveller and hunter, summing up an account of his position as he composed himself to rest upon a certain evening after a hard day's work. And no doubt it must have been very disagreeable. The night was cold and dark; and the intrepid traveller had to lie down to sleep in the open air, without even a tree to shelter him. A heavy shower of hail was falling; each hailstone about the size of an egg. The dark air was occasionally illuminated by forked lightning, of the most appalling aspect; and the thunder was deafening. By various sounds, heard in the intervals of the peals, it seemed evident that the vicinity was pervaded by wolves, tigers, elephants, wild boars, and serpents. A peculiar motion, perceptible under a horsecloth which was wrapped up to serve as a pillow, appeared to indicate that a snake was wriggling about underneath it. The hunter had some ground for thinking that it was a very venomous one; as indeed in the morning it proved to be; but he was too tired to look. And speaking of the general condition of matters upon that evening, the hunter stated, with great mildness of language, that "it was very disagreeable."

Most readers would be disposed to say, that disagreeable was hardly the right word. No doubt, all things that are perilous, horrible, awful, ghastly, deadly and the like, are disagreeable too. But when we use the word *disagreeable* by itself, our meaning is understood to be, that in calling the thing disagreeable, we have said the worst of it. A long and tiresome sermon is disagreeable; but a venomous snake under your pillow passes beyond being disagreeable. To have a tooth stopped, is disagreeable; to be broken on the wheel (though nobody could like it), transcends *that.* If a thing be horrible and awful, you would not say it was disagreeable. The greater includes the less; as when a human being becomes entitled to write D. D. after his name, he drops all mention of the M. A. borne in preceding years.

Let this truth be remembered, by such as shall read the following pages. We are to think about Disagreeable People. Let it be understood that (speaking generally) we are to think of people who are no worse than disagreeable. It cannot be denied, even by the most prejudiced, that murderers, pirates, slave-drivers, and burglars, are disagreeable. The cut-throat; the poisoner; the sneaking blackguard who shoots his landlord from behind a hedge, are no doubt disagreeable people; so very disagreeable that in this country the common consent of mankind removes them from human society by the instrumentality of a halter. But disagreeable is too mild a word. Such people are all that, and a great deal more. And accordingly, they stand beyond the range of this dissertation. We are to treat of folk who are disagreeable; and not worse than disagreeable. We may sometimes, indeed, overstep the boundary line. But it is to be remembered, that there are people who in the main are good people, who yet are extremely disagreeable. And a farther complication is introduced into the subject by the fact, that some people who are far from good, are yet unquestionably agreeable. You disapprove them; but you cannot help liking them. Others, again, are substantially good; yet you are angry with yourself to find that you cannot like them.

I take for granted that all observant human beings will admit that in this world there are disagreeable people. Probably the distinction which presses itself most strongly upon our attention as we mingle in the society of our fellow-men, is the distinction between agreeable people and disagreeable. There are various tests, more or less important, which put all mankind to right and left. A familiar division is into rich and poor. Thomas Paine, with great vehemence, denied the propriety of that classification; and declared that the only true and essential classification of mankind is into male and female. I have read a story whose author maintained, that, to his mind, by far the most interesting and thorough division of our race is into such as have been hanged and such as have not been hanged; he himself belonging to the former class. But we all, more or less, recognize and act upon the great classification of all human beings into the agreeable and the disagreeable. And we begin very early to recognize and act upon it. Very early in life, the little child understands and feels the vast difference between people who are nice, and people who are not nice. In schoolboy days, the first thing settled as to any new acquaintance, man or boy, is on which side he stands of the great boundary line. It is not genius, not scholarship, not wisdom, not strength nor speed, that fixes the man's place. None of these things is chiefly looked to; the question is, Is he agreeable or disagreeable? And according as that question is decided, the man is described, in the forcible language of youth, as "a brick," or as "a beast."

Yet it is to be remembered, that the division between the agreeable and disagreeable of mankind, is one which may be transcended. It is a scratch on the earth; not a ten-foot wall. And you will find men who pass from one side of it to the other; and back again; probably several times in a week, or even in a day. There are people whom you never know where to have. They are constantly skipping from side to side of that line of demarcation; or they even walk along with a foot on each side of it. There are people who are always disagreeable; and disagreeable to all men. There are people who are agreeable at some times, and disagreeable at others. There are people who are agreeable to some men and disagreeable to other men. I do not intend by the last-named class, people who intentionally make themselves agreeable to a certain portion of the race, to which they think it worth while to make themselves agreeable; and who do not take that trouble in the case of the remainder of humankind. What I mean is this: that there are people who have such an affinity and sympathy with certain other people; who so *suit* certain other people; that they are agreeable to these other people; though perhaps not particularly so to the race at large. And exceptional tastes and likings are often the strongest. The thing you like enthusiastically, another man absolutely loathes. The thing which all men like, is for the most part liked with a mild and subdued liking. Everybody likes good and well-made bread; but nobody goes into raptures over it. Few persons like caviare; but those who like it are very fond of it. I never knew but one being who liked mustard with apple-pie; but that solitary man ate it with avidity, and praised the flavor with enthusiasm.

But it is impossible to legislate for every individual case. Every rule must have exceptions from it; but it would be foolish to resolve to lay down no more rules. There may be, somewhere, the man who likes Mr. Snarling; and to that man Mr. Snarling would doubtless be agreeable. But for practical purposes, Mr. Snarling may justly be described as a disagreeable man, if he be disagreeable to nine hundred and ninety-nine mortals out of every thousand. And with precision sufficient for the ordinary business of life, we may say that there are people who are essentially disagreeable.

There are people who go through life, leaving an unpleasant influence on all whom they come near. You are not at your ease in their society. You feel awkward and constrained while with them. *That* is probably the mildest degree in the scale of unpleasantness. There are people who disseminate a much worse influence. As the upas-tree was said to blight all the country round it, so do these disagreeable folk prejudicially affect the whole surrounding moral atmosphere. They chill all warmth of heart in those near them; they put down anything generous or magnanimous; they suggest unpleasant thoughts and associations; they excite a diverse and numerous array of bad tempers. The great evil of disagreeable people lies in this: that they tend powerfully to make other people disagreeable too. And these people are not necessarily bad people, though they produce a bad effect. It is not certain that they design to be disagreeable. There are those who do entertain that design; and they always succeed in carrying it out.

Nobody ever tried diligently to be disagreeable, and failed. Such persons may indeed inflict much less annoyance than they wished, they may even fail of inflicting any pain whatever on others; but they make themselves as disgusting as they could desire. And in many cases, they succeed in inflicting a good deal of pain. A very low, vulgar, petty, and uncultivated nature, may cause much suffering to a lofty, noble, and refined one; particularly if the latter be in a position of dependence or subjection. A wretched hornet may madden a noble horse; a contemptible mosquito may destroy the night's rest which would have recruited a noble brain. But without any evil intention; sometimes with the very kindest intention; there are those who worry and torment you. It is through want of perception; want of tact; coarseness of nature; utter lack of power to understand you. Were you ever sitting in a considerable company, a good deal saddened by something you did not choose to tell to any one, and probably looking dull and dispirited enough; and did a fussy host or hostess draw the attention of the entire party upon you, by earnestly and repeatedly asking if you were ill, if you had a headache, because you seemed so dull and so unlike yourself? And did that person time after time return to the charge, till you would have liked to poison him? There is nothing more disagreeable, and few things more mischievous, than a well-meaning, meddling fool. And where there was no special intention, good or bad, towards yourself, you have known people make you uncomfortable through the simple exhibition to you, and pressure upon you, of their own inherent disagreeableness. You have known people after talking to whom for awhile, you felt disgusted with everything; and above all, with those people themselves. Talking to them, you felt your moral nature being rubbed against the grain; being stung all over with nettles. You showed your new house and furniture to such a man; and with eagle eye he traced out and pointed out every scratch on your fine fresh paint, and every flaw in your oak and walnut. He showed you that there were corners of your big mirrors that distort your face; that there were bits of your grand marble mantel-pieces that might be expected soon to scale away. Or you have known a man who, with no evil intention, made it his practice to talk of you before your face, as your other friends are accustomed to talk of you behind your back. It need not be said that the result is anything but pleasant. "What a fool you were, Smith, in saying *that* at Snooks's last night," your friend exclaims when you meet him next morning. You were quite aware, by this time, that what you said was foolish; but there is something grating in hearing your name connected with the unpleasant name. I would strongly advise any man, who does not wish to be set down as disagreeable, entirely to break off the habit (if he has such a habit) of addressing to even his best friends any sentence beginning with "What a fool you were." Let me offer the like advice as to sentences which set out as follows: "I say, Smith, I think your brother is the greatest fool on the face of the earth." Stop that kind of thing, my friend; or you may come to be classed with Mr. Snarling. You are probably a manly fellow, and a sincere friend; and for the sake of your substantial good qualities, one would stand a great deal. But over-frankness is disagreeable; and if you make over-frankness your leading characteristic, of course your entire character will come to be a disagreeable one; and you will be a disagreeable person.

Besides the people who are disagreeable through malignant intention, and through deficiency of sensitiveness, there are other people who are disagreeable through pure ill-luck. It is quite certain that there are people whom evil fortune dogs through all their life: who are thoroughly and hopelessly unlucky. And in no respect have we beheld a man's ill-luck so persecute him, as in the matter of making him (without the slightest evil purpose, and even when he is most anxious to render himself agreeable), render himself extremely disagreeable. Of course there must be some measure of thoughtlessness and forgetfulness; some lack of that social caution so indispensable in the complication of modern society, which teaches a man (so to speak) to try if the ice will bear him before venturing his entire weight upon it; about people who are unlucky in the way of which I am speaking. But doubtless you have known persons who were always saying disagreeable things, or putting disagreeable questions; either through forgetfulness of things which they ought to have remembered, or through unhappily chancing on forbidden ground. You will find a man, a thoughtless but quite good-natured man, begin at a dinner-table to relate a succession of stories very much to the prejudice of somebody; while somebody's daughter is sitting opposite him. And you will find the man quite obtuse to all the hints by which the host or hostess tries to stop him; and going on to particulars worse and worse; till in terror of what all this might grow to, the hostess has to exclaim, "Mr. Smith, you won't take a hint; *that* is Mr. Somebody's daughter sitting opposite you." It is quite essential that any man, whose conversation consists mainly of observations not at all to the advantage of some absent acquaintance, should carefully feel his way before giving full scope to his malice and his invention, in the presence of any general company. And before making any playful reference to halters, you should be clear that you are not talking to a man whose grandfather was hanged. Nor should you venture any depreciatory remarks upon men who have risen from the ranks, unless you are tolerably versed in the family history of those to whom you are talking. You may have heard a man very jocular upon lunatic asylums, to another who had several brothers and sisters in one. And though in some cases, human beings may render themselves disagreeable through a combination of circumstances which really absolves them from all blame; yet, as a general rule, the man who is disagreeable through ill-luck is at least guilty of culpable carelessness.

You have probably, my reader, known people who had the faculty of making themselves extremely agreeable. You have known one or two men who, whenever you met them, conveyed to you by a remarkably frank and genial manner, an impression that they esteemed you as one of their best and dearest friends. A vague idea took possession of your mind, that they had been longing to see you ever since they saw you last: which in all probability was six or twelve months previously. And during all that period it may be regarded as quite certain, that the thought of you had never once entered their mind. Such a manner has a vast effect upon young and inexperienced folk. The inexperienced man fancies that this manner, so wonderfully frank and friendly, is reserved specially for himself; and is a recognition of his own special excellences. But the man of greater experience has come to suspect this manner, and to see through it. He has discovered that it is the same to everybody: at least, to everybody to whom it is thought worth while to put it on. And he no more thinks of arguing the existence of any particular liking for himself, or of any particular merit in himself, from that friendly manner; than he thinks of believing, on a warm summer day, that the sun has a special liking for himself, and is looking so beautiful and bright all for himself. It is perhaps unjust to accuse the man, always overflowing in geniality upon everybody he meets, of being an impostor or humbug. Perhaps he does feel an irrepressible gush of love to all his race; but why convey to each individual of the race that he loves *him* more than all the others?

Yet it is to be admitted, that it is always well that a man should be agreeable. Pleasantness is always a pleasing thing. And a sensible man, seeking by honest means to make himself agreeable, will generally succeed in making himself agreeable to sensible men. But although there is an implied compliment, to your power if not to your personality, in the fact of a man's taking pains to make himself agreeable to you; it is certain that he may try to make himself so by means of which the upshot will be, to make him intensely disagreeable. You know the fawning, sneaking manner which an occasional shopkeeper adopts. It is most disagreeable to right-thinking people. Let him remember that he is also a man; and let his manner be manly as well as civil. It is an awful and humiliating sight, a man who is always squeezing himself together like a whipped dog whenever you speak to him; grinning and bowing; and (in a moral sense) wriggling about before you on the earth, and begging you to wipe your feet on his head. You cannot help thinking that the sneak would be a tyrant if he had the opportunity. It is pleasant to find people in the humblest position, blending a manly independence of demeanor with the regard justly due to those placed by Providence farther up the social scale. Yet doubtless there are persons to whom the sneakiest manner is agreeable; who enjoy the flattery and the humiliation of the wretched toady who is always ready to tell them that they are the most beautiful, graceful, witty, well-informed, aristocratic-looking, and generally-beloved, of the human race. You must remember that it depends very much upon the nature of a man himself, whether any particular demeanor shall be agreeable to him or not. And you know well that a cringing, toadying manner, which would be thoroughly disgusting to a person of sense, may be extremely agreeable and delightful to a self-conceited idiot. Was there not an idiotic monarch, who was greatly pleased when his courtiers, in speaking to him, affected to veil their eyes with their hands, as unable to bear the insufferable effulgence of his countenance? And would not a monarch of sense have been ready to kick the people who thus treated him like a fool? And every one has observed that there are silly women who are much gratified by coarse and fulsome compliments upon their personal appearance, which would be regarded as grossly insulting by a woman of sense. You may have heard of country gentlemen, of Radical politics, who had seldom wandered beyond their paternal acres (by their paternal acres I mean the acres they had recently bought), and who had there grown into a fixed belief that they were among the noblest and mightiest of the earth; who thought their parish clergyman an agreeable man if he voted at the county election for the candidate they supported, though that candidate's politics were directly opposed to those of the parson. These individuals, of course, would hold their clergyman as a disagreeable man, if he held by his own principles; and quite declined to take their wishes into account in exercising the trust of the franchise. Now of course a nobleman or gentleman of right feeling, would regard the parson as a turncoat and sneak, who should thus deny his convictions. Yes: there is no doubt that you may make yourself agreeable to unworthy folk, by unworthy means. A late notorious Marquis declared on his dying bed, that a two-legged animal of human pretensions, who had acted as his valet, and had aided that hoary reprobate in the gratification of his peculiar tastes, was "an excellent man." And you may remember how Burke said that as we learn that a certain Mr. Russell made himself very agreeable to Henry the Eighth, we may reasonably suppose that Mr. Russell was himself (in a humble degree) something like his master. Proba bly to most right-minded men, the fact that a man was agreeable to Henry the Eighth, or to the Marquis in question, or to Belial, Beelzebub, or Apollyon, would tend to make that man remarkably disagreeable. And let the reader remember the guarded way in which the writer laid down his general principle as to pleasantness of character and demeanor. I said that a sensible man, seeking by honest means to make himself agreeable, will generally succeed in making himself agreeable to sensible men. I exclude from the class of men to be esteemed agreeable, those who would disgust all but fools or blackguards. I exclude parsons who express heretical views in theology, in the presence of a patron known to be a free-thinker. I exclude men who do great folk's dirty work. I exclude all toad-eaters, sneaks, flatterers, and fawning impostors; from the schoolboy who thinks to gain his master's favor by voluntarily bearing tales of his companions, up to the bishop who declared that he regarded it not merely as a constitutional principle but as an ethical fact, that the King could do no wrong; and the other bishop who declared that the reason why George the Second died, was that this world was not good enough for him, and it was necessary to transfer him to heaven that he might be the right man in the right place. Such persons may succeed in making themselves agreeable to the man with whom they desire to ingratiate themselves, provided that man be a fool or a knave; but they assuredly render themselves disagreeable, not to say revolting, to all human beings whose good opinion is worth the possessing. And though any one who is not a fool will generally make himself agreeable to people of ordinary temper and nervous system if he wishes to do so; it is to be remembered that too intrusive attempts to be agreeable often make a man very disagreeable; and likewise, that a man is the reverse of agreeable if you see that he is trying by managing and humoring you to make himself agreeable to you. I mean, if you can see that he is smoothing you down, and agreeing with you, and trying to get you on your blind side, as if he thought you a baby or a lunatic. And there is all the difference in the world, between the frank hearty wish in man or woman to be agreeable; and this diplomatic and indirect way. No man likes to think that he is being managed as Mr. Rarey might manage an unbroken colt. And though many human beings must in fact be thus managed; though a person of a violent or a sullen temper, or of a wrong head, or of outrageous vanity, or of invincible prejudices, must be managed very much as you would manage a lunatic (being, in fact, removed from perfect sanity upon these points); still, they must never be allowed to discern that they *are* being managed; or the charm will fail at once. I confess, for myself, that I am no believer in the efficacy of diplomacy and indirect ways in dealing with one's fellow-creatures. I believe that a manly, candid, straightforward course is always the best.

Treat people in a perfectly frank manner: with frankness not put on, but real; and you will be agreeable to most of those to whom you would desire to be so.

My reader, I am now about to tell you of certain sorts of human beings, who appear to me as worthy of being ranked among disagreeable people. I do not pretend to give you an exhaustive catalogue of such. Doubtless you have your own black beasts, your own special aversions, which have for you a disagreeableness beyond the understanding or sympathy of others. Nor do I make quite sure that you will agree with me in all the views which I am going to set forth. It is not impossible that you may regard as very nice people, or even as quite fascinating and enthralling people, certain people whom I regard as intensely disagreeable. Let me begin with an order of human beings, as to which I do not expect every one who reads this page to go along with me; though I do not know any opinion which I hold more resolutely than that which I am about to express.

We all understand the kind of thing which is meant by people who talk of *Muscular Christianity.* It is certainly a noble and excellent thing to make people discern that a good Christian need not be a muff (pardon the slang term: there is no other that would bring out my meaning). It is a fine thing to make it plain that manliness and dash may coexist with pure morality and sincere piety. It is a fine thing tc make young fellows comprehend that there is nothing fine and manly in being bad; and nothing unmanly in being good. And in this view, it is impossible to value too highly such characters and such biographies as those of Hodson of Hodson's Horse and of Captain Hedley Vicars. It is a splendid combination, pluck and daring in their highest degree, with an unaffected and earnest regard to religion and religious duties: in short, muscularity with Christianity. A man consists of body and soul: and both would be in their ideal perfection, if the soul were decidedly Christian, and the body decidedly muscular.

But there are folk whose admiration of the muscularity is very great; but whose regard for the Christianity is very small. They are captivated by the dash and glitter of physical pluck; they are quite content to accept it without any Christianity; and even without the most ordinary morality and decency. They appear, indeed, to think that the grandeur of the character is increased, by the combination of thorough blackguardism with high physical qualifications; their gospel, in short, may be said to be that of *Unchristian Muscularity.* And you will find various books in which the hero is such a man; and while the writer of the book frankly admits that he is in strict morality an extremely bad man, the writer still recalls his doings with such manifest gusto and sympathy, and takes such pains to make him agreeable on the whole, and relates with such approval the admiration which empty-headed idiots express for him when he has jumped his horse over some very perilous fence or thrashed some insolent farmer, that it is painfully apparent what is the writer's ideal of a grand and imposing character. You know the kind of man who is the hero of some novels: the muscular blackguard; and you remember what are his unfailing characteristics. He has a deep chest. He has huge arms and limbs: the muscles being knotted. He has an immense moustache. He has (God knows why) a serene contempt for ordinary mortals. He is always growing black with fury, and bullying weak men. On such occasions, his lips may be observed to be twisted into an evil sneer. He is a seducer and liar: he has ruined various women, and had special facilities for becoming acquainted with the rottenness of society; and occasionally he expresses, in language of the most profane, not to say blasphemous character, a momentary regret for having done so much harm; such as the Devil might sentimentally have expressed when he had succeeded in misleading our first parents. Of course he never pays tradesmen for the things with which they supply him. He can drink an enormous quantity of wine without his head becoming affected. He looks down with entire disregard on the laws of God and man, as made for inferior beings. As for any worthy moral quality; as for anything beyond a certain picturesque brutality and bull-dog disregard of danger; not a trace of such a thing can be found about him.

We all know, of course, that such a person, though not uncommon in novels, very rarely occurs in real life; and if he occur at all, it is with his ideal perfections very much toned down. In actual life, such a hero would become known in the Insolvent Court, and would frequently appear before the police magistrates. He would eventually become a billiard-marker; and might ultimately be hanged, with general approval. If the man, in his unclipped proportions, did actually exist, it would be right that a combination should be formed to wipe him out of creation. He should be put down : as you would put down a tiger or a rattlesnake if found at liberty somewhere in the Midland Counties. A more hateful character, to all who possess a grain of moral discernment, could not even be imagined. And it need not be shown, that the conception of such a character is worthy only of a baby. However many years the man who deliberately and admiringly delineates such a person may have lived in this world, intellectually he cannot be more than about seven years old. And none but calves the most immature can possibly sympathize with him. Yet if there were not many silly persons to whom such a character is agreeable, such a character would not be portrayed. And it seems certain that a single exhibition of strength or daring will to some minds be the compendium of all good qualities: or (more accurately speaking) the equivalent for them. A muscular blackguard clears a high fence; he does precisely that, neither more nor less. And upon the strength of that single achievement, the servants of the house where he is visiting declare that they would follow him over the world. And you may find various young women, and various women who wish to pass for young, who would profess, and perhaps actually feel, a like enthusiasm for the muscular blackguard. I confess that I cannot find words strong enough to express my contempt and abhorrence for the theory of life and character which is assumed by the writers who describe such blackguards, and by the fools who admire them. And though very far from saying or thinking that the kind of human being who has been described, is no worse than disagreeable, I assert with entire confidence that to all right-thinking men, he is more disagreeable than almost any other kind of human being. And I do not know any single lesson you could instil into a youthful mind, which would be so mischievous, as the lesson that the muscular blackguard should be regarded with any other feeling than that of pure loathing and disgust. But let us have done with him. I cannot think of the books which delineate him, and ask you to admire him, without indignation more bitter than I wish to feel in writing such a page.

And passing to the consideration of human beings who though disagreeable, are good in the main; it may be laid down, as a general principle, that any person, however good, is disagreeable, from whom you feel it a relief to get away. We have all known people, thoroughly estimable, and whom you could not but respect, in whose presence it was impossible to feel at ease; and whose absence was felt as the withdrawal of a sense of constraint of the most oppressive kind. And this vague, uncomfortable influence, which breathes from some men, is produced in various ways. Sometimes it is the result of mere stiffness and awkwardness of manner; and there are men whose stiffness and awkwardness of manner are such as would freeze the most genial and silence the frankest. Sometimes it arises from ignorance of social rules and proprieties; sometimes from incapacity to take, or even to comprehend, a joke. Sometimes it proceeds from a pettedness of nature, which keeps you ever in fear that offence may be taken at the most innocent word or act. Sometimes it comes of a preposterous sense of his own standing and importance, existing in a man whose standing and importance are very small. It is quite wonderful what very great folk, very little folk will sometimes fancy themselves to be. The present writer has had little opportunity of conversing with men of great rank and power. Yet he has conversed with certain men of the very greatest; and he can say sincerely that he has found head-stewards to be much more dignified men than dukes; and parsons of no earthly reputation, and of very limited means, to be infinitely more stuck-up than archbishops. And though at first the airs of stuck-up small men are amazingly ridiculous, and so rather amusing; they speedily become so irritating, that the men who exhibit them cannot be classed otherwise than with the disagreeable of the earth.

Few people are more disagreeable than the man who (you know) is, while you are conversing with him, taking a mental estimate of you; more particularly of the soundness of your doctrinal views; with the intention of showing you up if you be wrong, and of inventing or misrepresenting something to your prejudice if you be right. Whenever you find any man trying (in a moral sense) to trot you out, and examine your paces, and pronounce upon your general soundness; there are two courses you may follow. The one is, severely to shut him up; and sternly make him understand that you don't choose to be inspected by him. Show him that you will not exhibit for his approval your particular views about the Papacy, or about Moral Inability, or about Pelagianism or the Patripassian heresy. Indicate that you will not be pumped; and you may convey, in a kindly and polite way, that you really don't care a rush what he thinks of you. The other course is, with deep solemnity and an unchanged countenance, to horrify your inspector by avowing the most fearful views. Tell him that on long reflection, you are prepared to advocate the revival of Cannibalism. Say that probably something may be said for Polygamy. Defend the Thugs, and say something for Mumbo Jumbo. End by saying that no doubt black is white, and twice ten are fifty. Or a third way of meeting such a man, is suddenly to turn upon him, and ask him to give you a brief and lucid account of the views he is condemning. Ask him to tell you what are the theological peculiarities of Bunsen; and what is the exact teaching of Mr. Maurice. He does not know, you may be tolerably sure. In the case of the latter eminent man, I never met anybody who did know; and I have the firmest belief that he does not know himself. I was told, lately, of an eminent foreigner, who came to Britain to promote a certain public end. For its promotion, the eminent man wished to conciliate the sympathies of a certain small class of religionists. He procured an introduction to a leading man among them; a good, but very stupid and self-conceited man. This man entered into talk with the eminent foreigner; and ranged over a multitude of topics, political and religious. And at an hour's end the foreigner was astonished by the good but stupid man suddenly exclaiming: "Now, sir, I have been reckoning you up; you won't do; you are a" — no matter what. It was something that had nothing earthly to do with the end to be promoted. The religious demagogue had been trotting out the foreigner; and he had found him unsound. The religious demagogue belonged to a petty sect, no doubt; and he was trying for his wretched little Shibboleth. But you may have seen the like, even with leading men in National Churches. And I have seen a pert little whippersnapper ask a venerable clergyman what he thought of a certain outrageous lay-preacher; and receive the clergyman's reply that he thought most unfavorably of many of the lay-preacher's doings, with a self-conceited smirk that seemed to say to the venerable clergyman, "I have been reckoning *you* up; you won't do."

People whom you cannot get to attend to you when you talk to them, are disagreeable. There are men whom you feel it is vain to speak to; whether you are mentioning facts, or stating arguments. All the while you are speaking, they are thinking of what they are themselves to say next. There is a strong current, as it were, setting outward from their minds; and it prevents what you say from getting in. You know, if a pipe be full of water, running strongly one way, it is vain to think to push in a stream running the other way. You cannot get at their attention. You cannot get at the quick of their mental sensorium. It is not the dull of hearing whom it is hardest to get to hear: it is rather the man who is roaring out himself, and so who cannot attend to anything else. Now this is provoking. It is a mortifying indication of the little importance that is attached to what we are saying; and there is something of the irritation that is produced in the living being by contending with the passive resistance of inert matter. And there is something provoking even in the outward signs that the mind is in a non-receptive state. You remember the eye that is looking beyond you; the grin that is not at anything funny in what you say; the occasional inarticulate sounds that are put in at the close of your sentences, as if to delude you with a show of attention. The non-receptive mind is occasionally found in clever men; but the men who exhibit it are invariably very conceited. They can think of nothing but themselves. And you may find the last-named characteristic strongly developed, even in men with gray hair, who ought to have learned better through the experience of a pretty long life. There are other minds which are very receptive. They seem to have a strong power of suction. They take in, very decidedly, all that is said to them. The best mind, of course, is that which combines both characteristics; which is strongly receptive when it ought to be receiving; and which gives out strongly when it ought to be giving out. The power of receptivity is greatly increased by habit. I remember feeling awe-stricken by the intense attention with which a very great Judge was wont, in ordinary conversation, to listen to all that was said to him. It was the habit of the judgment-seat, acquired through many years of listening, with every faculty awake, to the arguments addressed to him. But when you began to make some statement to him, it was positively alarming to see him look you full in the face, and listen with inconceivable fixedness of attention to all you said. You could not help feeling that really the small remark you had to make was not worth that great mind's grasping it so intently, as he might have grasped an argument by Follett. The mind was intensely receptive, when it was receiving at all. But I remember, too, that when the great Judge began to speak, then his mind was, (so to speak,) streaming out; and he was particularly impatient of inattention or interruption; and particularly non-receptive of anything that might be suggested to him.

It is extremely disagreeable when a vulgar fellow, whom you hardly know, addresses you by your surname with great familiarity of manner. And such a person will take no hint that he is disagreeable; however stiff, and however formally polite, you may take pains to be to him. It is disagreeable when persons, with whom you have no desire to be on terms of intimacy, persist in putting many questions to you as to your private concerns; such as your annual income and expenditure, and the like. No doubt, it is both pleasant and profitable for people who are not rich, to compare notes on these matters with some frank and hearty friend, whose means and outgoings are much the same as their own. I do not think of such a case; but of the prying curiosity of persons who have no right to pry, and who, very generally, while diligently prying into your affairs, take special care not to take you into their confidence. Such people, too, while making a pretence of revealing to you all their secrets, will often tell a very small portion of them, and make various statements which you at the time are quite aware are not true. There are not many things more disagreeable than a very stupid and ill-set old woman, who, quite unaware what her opinion is worth, expresses it with entire confidence upon many subjects of which she knows nothing whatever, and as to which she is wholly incapable of judging. And the self-satisfied and confident air with which she settles the most difficult questions, and pronounces unfavorable judgment upon people ten thousand times wiser and better than herself, is an insufferably irritating phenomenon. It is a singular fact, that the people I have in view invariably combine extreme ugliness with spitefulness and self-conceit. Such a person will make particular inquiries of you as to some near relative of your own; and will add, with a malicious and horribly ugly expression of face, that she is glad to hear how *very much improved* your relative now is. She will repeat the sentence several times, laying great emphasis and significance upon the *very much improved.* Of course, the notion conveyed to any stranger who may be present, is that your relative must in former days have been an extremely bad fellow. The fact probably is, that he has always, man and boy, been particularly well-behaved; and that really you were not aware that he needed any special improvement; save indeed in the sense that every human being might be and ought to be a great deal better than he is.

People who are always vaporing about their own importance, and the value of their own possessions, are disagreeable. We all know such people; and they are made more irritating by the fact, that their boasting is almost invariably absurd and false. I do not mean ethically false, but logically false. For doubtless, in many cases, human beings honestly think themselves and their possessions as much better than other men and their possessions; as they say they do. If thirty families compose the best society of a little country town, you may be sure that each of the thirty families in its secret soul looks down upon the other twenty-nine; and fancies that it stands on a totally different level. And it is a kind arrangement of Providence, that a man's own children, horses, house, and other possessions, are so much more interesting to himself than are the children, horses, and houses of other men, that he can readily persuade himself that they are as much better in fact, as they are more interesting to his personal feeling. But it is provoking when a man is always obtruding on you how highly he estimates his own belongings, and how much better than yours he thinks them, even when this is done in all honesty and simplicity; and it is infuriating when a man keeps constantly telling you things which he knows are not true, as to the preciousness and excellence of the gifts with which fortune has endowed him. You feel angry when a man, who has lately bought a house, one in a square containing fifty, all as nearly as possible alike, tells you with an air of confidence that he has got the finest house in Scotland, or in England, as the case may be. You are irritated by the man who on all occasions tells you that he drives in his mail-phaeton "five hundred pounds' worth of horseflesh." You are well aware that he did not pay a quarter of that sum for the animals in question; and you assume as certain that the dealer did not give him that pair of horses for less than they were worth. It is somewhat irritating when a man, not remarkable in any way, begins to tell you that he can hardly go to any part of the world without being recognized by some one who remembers his striking aspect, or is familiar with his famous name. "It costs me three hundred a year, having that picture to look at," said Mr. Windbag, pointing to a picture hanging on a wall in his library. He goes on to explain that he refused six thousand pounds for that picture; which at five per cent. would yield the annual income named. You repeat Windbag's statement to an eminent artist. The artist knows the picture. He looks at you fixedly; and for all comment on Windbag's story, says (he is a Scotchman) HOOT TOOT. But the disposition to vapor is deep set in human nature. There are not very many men or women whom I would trust, to give an accurate account of their family, dwelling, influence, and general position, to people a thousand miles from home, who were not likely ever to be able to verify the picture drawn.

It is hardly necessary to mention among disagreeable people, those individuals who take pleasure in telling you that you are looking ill; that you are falling off, physically or mentally. "Surely you have lost some of your teeth since I saw you last," said a good man to a man of seventy-five years: "I cannot make out a word you say, you speak so indistinctly." And so obtuse, and so thoroughly devoid of gentlemanly feeling, was that good man, that when admonished that he ought not to speak in that fashion to a man in advanced years, he could not for his life see that he had done anything unkind or unmannerly. "I dare say you are wearied wi' preachin' to-day; you see you're gettin' frail noo," said a Scotch *elder*, in my hearing, to a worthy clergyman. Seldom has it cost me a greater effort than it did to refrain from turning to the elder, and saying with candor, "What a boor and what a fool *you* must be, to say *that!*" It was as well I did not; the boor would not have known what I meant. He would not have known the provocation which led me to give him my true opinion of him. "How very bald you are getting," said a really good-natured man, to a friend he was meeting for the first time in several years. Such remarks are for the most part made by men who, in good faith, have not the least idea that they are making themselves disagreeable. There is no malicious intention. It is a matter of pure obtuseness, stupidity, selfishness, and vulgarity. But an obtuse, stupid, selfish, and vulgar person is disagreeable. And your right course will be, to carefully avoid all intercourse with such a person.

But besides people who blunder into saying unpleasant things, there are a few who do so of set intention. And such people ought to be cracked. They can do a great deal of harm; inflict a great deal of suffering. I believe that human beings in general are more miserable than you think. They are very anxious; very careworn; stung by a host of worries; a good deal disappointed, in many ways. And in the case of many people, worthy and able, there is a very low estimate of themselves and their abilities; and a sad tendency to depressed spirits and gloomy views. And while a kind word said to such is a real benefit, and a great lightener of the heart; an ingenious malignant may suggest to such, things which are as a stunning blow, and as an added load on the weary frame and mind. I have seen, with burning indignation, a malignant beast (I mean man) playing upon that tendency to a terrible apprehensiveness which is born with many men. I have seen the beast vaguely suggest evil to the nervous and apprehensive man. "This cannot end here;" "I shall take my own measures now;" "A higher authority shall decide between us;" I have heard the beast say; and then go away. Of course I knew well that the beast could and would do nothing; and I hastened to say so to the apprehensive man. But I knew that the poor fellow would go away home; and brood over the beast's ominous threats; and imagine a hundred terrible contingencies; and work himself into a fever of anxiety and alarm. And it is because I know that the vague threatener counted on all that; and wished it; and enjoyed the thought of the slow torment he was causing; that I choose to call him a beast rather than a man. Indeed, there is an order of beings, worse than beasts, to which that being should rather be referred. You have said or done something, which has given offence to certain of your neighbors. Mr. Snarling comes and gives you a full and particular account of the indignation they feel, and of their plans for vengeance. Mr. Snarling is happy to see you look somewhat annoyed; and he kindly says, "Oh, never mind; this will blow over, as *other things you have said and done have blown over.*" Thus he vaguely suggests that you have given great offence on many occasions, and made many bitter enemies. He adds, in a musing voice, "Yes, as MANY other things have blown over." Turn the individual out; and cut his acquaintance. It would be better to have a upas-tree in your neighborhood. Of all disagreeable men, a man with his tendencies is the most disagreeable. The bitterest and longest lasting east wind, acts less perniciously on body and soul, than does the society of Mr. Snarling.

Suspicious people are disagreeable, also people who are always taking the pet. Indeed, suspiciousness and pettedness generally go together. There are many men and women who are always imagining that some insult is designed by the most innocent words and doings of those around them; and always suspecting that some evil intention against their peace is cherished by some one or other. It is most irritating to have anything to do with such impracticable and silly mortals. But it is a delightful thing to work along with a man who never takes offence: a frank, manly man, who gives credit to others for the same generosity of nature which he feels within himself; and who if he thinks he has reason to complain, speaks out his mind and has things cleared up at once. A disagreeable person is he who frequently sends letters to you without paying the postage; leaving you to pay twopence for each penny which he has thus saved. The loss of twopence is no great matter; but there is something irritating in the feeling that your correspondent has deliberately resolved that he would save his penny at the cost of your twopence. There is a man, describing himself as a clergyman of the Church of England, (I cannot think he is one,) who occasionally sends me an abusive anonymous letter, and who invariably sends his letters unpaid. I do not mind about the man's abuse, but I confess I grudge my twopence. I have observed, too, that the people who send letters unpaid do so habitually. I have known the same individual send six successive letters unpaid. And it is probably within the experience of most of my readers, that out of (say) a hundred correspondents, ninety-nine invariably pay their letters properly; while time after time the hundredth sends his with the abominable big 2 stamped upon it, and your servant walks in and worries you by the old statement that the postman is waiting. Let me advise every reader to do what I intend doing for the future: to wit, to refuse to receive any unpaid letter. You may be quite sure that by so doing you will not lose any letter that is worth having. A class of people, very closely analogous to that of the people who do not pay their letters is that of such as are constantly borrowing small sums from their friends, which they never restore. If you should ever be thrown into the society of such, your right course will be to take care to have no money in your pocket. People are disagreeable, who are given to talking of the badness of their servants, the undutifulness of their children, the smokiness of their chimneys, and the deficiency of their digestive organs. And though with a true and close friend, it is a great relief, and a special tie, to have spoken out your heart about your burdens and sorrows, it is expedient, in conversation with ordinary acquaintances, to keep these to yourself.

It must be admitted, with great regret, that people who make a considerable profession of religion have succeeded in making themselves more thoroughly disagreeable than almost any other human beings have ever made themselves. You will find people, who not merely claim to be pious and Christian people, but to be very much more pious and Christian than others, who are extremely uncharitable, unamiable, repulsive, stupid, and narrow-minded; and intensely opinionated and self-satisfied. We know, from a very high authority, that a Christian ought to be an epistle in commendation of the blessed faith he holds. But it is beyond question, that many people who profess to be Christians, are like grim Gorgon's heads warning people off from having anything to do with Christianity. Why should a middle-aged clergyman walk about the streets with a sullen and malignant scowl always on his face, which at the best would be a very ugly one? Why should another walk with his nose in the air, and his eyes rolled up till they seem likely to roll out? And why should a third be always dabbled over with a clammy perspiration, and prolong all his vowels to twice the usual length? It is indeed a most woful thing, that people who evince a spirit in every respect the direct contrary of that of our Blessed Redeemer, should fancy that they are Christians of singular attainments; and it is more woful still, that many young people should be scared away into irreligion or unbelief by the wretched delusion that these creatures, wickedly caricaturing Christianity, are fairly representing it. I have beheld more deliberate malice, more lying and cheating, more backbiting and slandering, denser stupidity, and greater self-sufficiency, among bad-hearted and wrong-headed religionists, than among any other order of human beings. I have known more malignity and slander conveyed in the form of a prayer, than should have consigned any ordinary libeller to the pillory. I have known a person who made evening prayer a means of infuriating and stabbing the servants, under the pretext of confessing their sins. "Thou knowest, Lord, how my servants have been occupied this day;" with these words did the blasphemous mockery of prayer begin one Sunday evening in a house I could easily indicate. And then the man, under the pretext of addressing the Almighty, raked up all the misdoings of the servants (they being present of course), in a fashion which, if he had ventured on it at any other time, would probably have led some of them to assault him. "I went to Edinburgh," said a Highland elder, "and was there a Sabbath. It was an awfu' sight? There, on the Sabbath-day, you would see people walking along the street, smiling AS IF THEY WERE PERFECTLY HAPPY!" There was the *gravamen* of the poor Highlander's charge. To think of people being or looking happy on the Lord's day! And indeed to think of a Christian man ever venturing to be happy at all! "Yes, this parish was highly favored in the days of Mr. Smith and Mr. Brown," said a spiteful and venomous old woman, — with a glance of deadly malice at a young lad who was present. That young lad was the son of the clergyman of the parish, — one of the most diligent and exemplary clergymen in Britain. Mr. Smith and Mr. Brown were the clergymen who preceded him. And the spiteful old woman adopted this means of sticking a pin into the young lad, conveying the idea that there was a sad falling off now. I saw and heard her, my reader. Now when an ordinary spiteful person says a malicious thing, being quite aware that she is saying a malicious thing, and that her motive is pure malice, you are disgusted. But when a spiteful person says a malicious thing, all the while fancying herself a very pious person, and fancying that in gratifying her spite, she is acting from Christian principle, I say the sight is to me one of the most disgusting, perplexing, and miserable, that ever human eye beheld. I have no fear of the attacks of enemies on the blessed Faith in which I live, and hope to die. But it is dismal, to see how our holy religion is misrepresented before the world, by the vile impostors who pretend to be its friends.

Among the disagreeable people who make a profession of religion, probably many are purely hypocrites. But we willingly believe that there are people, in whom Christianity appears in a wretchedly stunted and distorted form, who yet are right at the root. It does not follow that a man is a Christian, because he turns up his eyes and drawls out his words; and when asked to say grace, offers a prayer of twenty minutes' duration. But again, it does not follow that he is *not* a Christian, though he may do all these things. The bitter sectary, who distinctly says that a humble, pious man, just dead, has "gone to hell," because he died in the bosom of the Church, — however abhorrent that sectary may be in some respects, — may be, in the main, within the Good Shepherd's fold, wherein he fancies there are very few but himself. The dissenting teacher who declared from his pulpit that the parish clergyman (newly come, and an entire stranger to him) was "a servant of Satan," may possibly have been a good man, after all. Grievous defects and errors may exist in a Christian character, which is a Christian character still. And the Christian, horribly disagreeable and repulsive now, will some day, we trust, have all *that* purged away. But I do not hesitate to say, that any Christian, by so far as he is disagreeable and repulsive, deviates from the right thing. Oh, my reader, when my heart is sometimes sore through what I see of disagreeable traits in Christian character, what a blessed relief there is in turning to the simple pages, and seeing for the thousandth time The True Christian Character, — so different! Yes, thank God, we know where to look, to find what every pious man should be humbly aiming to be; and when we see That Face, and hear That Voice, there is something that soothes and cheers among the wretched imperfections (in one's self as in others), of the present: — something that warms the heart, and that brings a man to his knees!

The present writer has a relative, who is Professor of Theology in a certain famous University. With that theologian I recently had a conversation on the matter of which we have just been thinking. The Professor lamented bitterly the unchristian features of character which may be found in many people making a great parade of their Christianity. He mentioned various facts, which had recently come to his own knowledge; which would sustain stronger expressions of opinion than any which I have given. But he went on to say, that it would be a sad thing if no fools could get to heaven; nor any unamiable, narrow-minded, sour, and stupid people. Now, said he, with great force of reason, religion does not alter idiosyncrasy. When a fool becomes a Christian, he will be a foolish Christian. A narrow-minded man will be a narrow-minded Christian; a stupid man, a stupid Christian. And though a malignant man will have his malignity much diminished, it by no means follows that it will be completely rooted out. "When I would do good, evil is present with me." "I find a law in my members, warring against the law of my mind; and enslaving me to the law of sin." But you are not to blame Christianity for the stupidity and unamiability of Christians. If they be disagreeable, it is not the measure of true religion they have got, that makes them so. In so far as they are disagreeable, they depart from the standard. You know, you may make water sweet or sour; you may make it red, blue, black; and it will be water still, though its purity and pleasantness are much interfered with. In like manner, Christianity may coexist with a good deal of acid, — with a great many features of character very inconsistent with itself. The cup of fair water may have a bottle of ink emptied into it, or a little verjuice, or even a little strychnine. And yet, though sadly deteriorated, though hopelessly disguised, the fair water is there; and not entirely neutralized.

And it is worth remarking, that you will find many persons who are very charitable to blackguards, but who have no charity for the weaknesses of really good people. They will hunt out the act of thoughtless liberality, done by the scapegrace who broke his mother's heart, and squandered his poor sisters' little portions; they will make much of that liberal act, — such an act as tossing to some poor Magdalen a purse, filled with money which was probably not his own; and they will insist that there is hope for the blackguard yet. But these persons will tightly shut their eyes against a great many substantially good deeds, done by a man who thinks Prelacy the abomination of desolation, or who thinks that stained glass and an organ are sinful. I grant you that there is a certain fairness in trying the blackguard and the religionist by different standards. Where the pretension is higher, the test may justly be more severe. But I say it is unfair to puzzle out with diligence the one or two good things in the character of a reckless scamp, and to refuse moderate attention to the many good points about a weak, narrow-minded, and uncharitable good person. I ask for charity in the estimating of all human characters, — even in estimating the character of the man who would show no charity to another. I confess freely that in the last-named case, the exercise of charity is extremely difficult.

CHAPTER VI.

OUTSIDE.

THERE is a tremendous difference between being Inside and being Outside. The distance in space may be very small; but the distance in feeling is vast. Sometimes the outside is the better place, sometimes the inside; but I have always thought that this is a case in which there is an interruption of nature's general law of gradation. Other differences are shaded off into each other. Youth passes imperceptibly into age; the evening light melts gradually into darkness; and you may find some mineral production to mark every step in the progress from lava to granite, which (as you probably do not know) are in their elements the same thing. But it is a positive and striking fact, that you are outside or inside. There is no gradation nor shading off between the two. I am sitting here on a green knoll; the ground slopes away steeply on three sides, down to a little river. The grass is very rich and fresh; and it is lighted up with innumerable buttercups and daisies. You can see that the old monks, who used to worship in that lovely Gothic chapel, brought these acres under cultivation in days when what is now the fertile country round, was a desolate waste. And the warm air of one of the last days of May is just stirring the thick trees around. But all this is because I am outside. There is an inside hard by where things are very different. Down below this green knoll, but on a rock high above the little river, you may see the ruins of an old feudal castle. Last night I passed over the narrow bridge that leads to the rock on which the ruins stand; and a young fellow, moderately versed in its history, showed me all that remains of the castle. You go away down, stair after stair, and reach successive ranges of chambers, all of stone, formerly guard-rooms and kitchens. These chambers are sufficiently cheerful; for though on one side far underground, on the other side they are high above the glen and the river. The setting sun was streaming into their windows; and the fresh green of beeches and pines looked over from the other side of the narrow gorge. But now the young fellow mentioned that the dungeons were still far beneath; and in a pitch-dark passage, he made me feel a small doorway, black as night, going down to the horrible dark recesses below, to which not a ray of light was admitted, and to which not a breath of the fragrant spring air without could ever come. You could not but think what it must have been, long ago, to be dragged through those dark passages, and violently thrust through that narrow door, and down to the black abyss. You felt how thoroughly hopeless escape would be, — how entirely you were at the mercy of the people who put you there. And coming up from those dungeons, climbing the successive stairs, you reached the daylight again; and descending the steep walks of the garden, you reached a place just outside the dungeons; which on this side are far above ground. There was the pleasant summer sunset; there were the milk-white hawthorns and the fragrant lilacs; there was an apple-tree, whose pink and white blossoms were gently swayed by the warm wind against the outside of the dungeon-wall. And, almost hidden by green leaves, you could hear the stream below, whose waters (it is to be confessed) had suffered somewhat from the presence, a few miles above, of various paper-mills. And here, I thought, were the outside and the inside; only six feet of wall between; but in all their aspect, and above all in the feeling of the crushed captive within, a thousand miles apart. Of course, there was no captive there now; but all this scene was the same in the days when those dungeons were fully inhabited. And doubtless, many of those who were then thrust into those dismal places liked them just as little as you and I should; and were missed and needed by some outside just as much as you or I could be.

In this case, you observe, it is better to be outside than to be inside. But there are many cases in which it is otherwise.

You may be outside physically; as you would be if you were to fall, unnoticed, and in the night, overboard from a ship, — and it to pass on, and leave you to perish in the black waters. Many human beings have done *that;* an old school-fellow of mine did. It must be a dreadful thing. It would be better, in such a case, not to be able to swim; for then the suffering would be the sooner over; and the mind would be in such a bewildered, hurried state, that there would be less room for the agony of thought. But in warmer seas, where the chill of the water would not speedily benumb into loss of power and consciousness, the single hour through which, as Cowper tells us, an unaided swimmer might sustain himself in life, would seem like a lifetime. I know a man who supported himself for a whole night, by the help of two oars, after his vessel had gone down in the Indian Ocean. His wife and child went with it; and after desperate efforts to save them, he found himself in the water, clinging to his two oars. Three times, through that awful night, he cast the oars away from him, and dived deep under the surface, hoping that he might never come up; but the instinctive clinging to life was too strong; and each time he faintly struggled back to his oars again.

Then you may be outside morally. You may somehow have turned out of the track in which those who started with you are going on in life. Perhaps through folly, perhaps through sin, you have got beyond the pale. There is a narrow passage in a certain city, a steep and narrow passage of evil odors, through which many clergymen are wont to go to a certain building, in which a great ecclesiastical council meets. In a dark recess, opening into that narrow passage, and leading to various wretched dwellings, I have beheld a deposed and degraded minister standing in the darkest shadow he could find, and watching those who were once his brethren going up by the way he once used to go, — but shrinking back from their notice. Alas for the poor outsider, — so near physically to the place where he used to be, but morally so far away! Surely his case is worse than that of the castaway, swept from the deck into the boiling ocean. After that sad instance, we shall feel the less sympathy for such moral outsiders as those who suffer through the existence of lines of social cleavage: the people who chafe at being excluded from the society of the great and exclusive First Circle of a little country town; or who complain keenly that some wealthy or perhaps noble neighbor keeps them on the outside of his dwelling. Probably you have known people feel this moral exclusion very bitterly. You may have heard a lady in some small community complain with extreme severity that she was thus made an outsider; and that, in the festive tea-parties which went on in the halls of light around her she was permitted to have no part. At the same time she probably showed, with great force of statement and argument, that she was in all respects a great deal better than the people inside that charmed circle to whose outside she was condemned. You could but sympathize with the individual in her sor row, and advise her not to mind. Every one has known the wrath and jealousies which have arisen from thus putting people morally outside, — from not sending them cards on the occasion of a marriage, — from not inviting them to some entertainment. You may remember a classical instance of the wrathful spirit awakened in a human being stung by the sense of being outside. Mr. Samuel Warren describes a man as standing in Hyde Park on an afternoon in the fashionable season, seeing all that gay life going on, and feeling that he had nothing to do with it, and bestowing on the whole system of things his extremest malison. Perhaps a worthier nature might have looked on in kindly interest at a class of concerns and a mode of existence in which he had no share; and hoped that all paths through this world, however far apart in time, might yet end and meet in the same happy place together. We may wish well, my reader, — and I trust we shall wish well, — even to those with whom we have little in common, — even to those beyond the circle of whose sympathies we stand, and beyond whose comprehension our great interests lie.

Moral outsideness may coexist with physical insideness. This truth is well known to unpopular officers in regiments, who though physically inside are morally outside; also to schoolboys who for some offence have been temporarily sent to Coventry by their young companions. And probably such find it a heavy trial to be placed outside the pale of society, — to sit on a form at school with thirty other boys, none of whom will speak to them, — to be cut off from joining in the games of the play-ground. There used to be a vulgar expression current among Scotch schoolboys, — probably it is current still, — which was founded on this principle: that a human being though physically an insider may be morally an outsider. You spoke of being *in with* such a youthful companion, and *out with* such another. You are aware how consignment to moral outsideness often serves as a fearful punishment of offences to which laws cannot reach. To be entirely repudiated and cast off by the society amid which you live, whether lofty or lowly, — to be made a social outlaw and outsider, — is something not easily borne even by the most callous; — something which right-thinking men could support only by the firm conviction that solemn principle prompted the conduct which brought down this reprobation. It is not nearly so lonely a thing to dwell in the wilderness, never seeing a human face, as it would be to live in the town in which you were born and brought up, and to see, as you walked its streets, scores of faces you know well, but each averted as you pass. You may have seen poor women bear this, with what crucifixion of the whole nature they only know; you may have beheld them face the unconsciousness of their presence on the part of old friends with a disdainful smile, or meet it with the look that betokened a breaking heart. I have witnessed this, my reader, more than once; and I doubt not you have done so too. As for men, they can stand all this better. *They* can always find a certain class who are content to associate with them: a class of people like themselves. And with a great injustice, not indeed without some reasons in its favor, you know how even the most reputable society passes lightly in a man what it visits with its severest reprobation in a woman. Yes; you may have witnessed a brazen outsider, who ought never to have been suffered inside again, gradually elbowing himself, by force of face, into weight in the senate of a certain moral country. You may have known an unrepenting blackguard, once cast out by the society of the town and the county, and who never afforded the faintest reason why he should be let in, step by step getting in again; till at length the aged reprobate was in high favor in families abounding in girls, and saw clergymen of great pretensions seated at his hospitable board. Yet, in the main, a man becomes an outsider by deserving it. I mean an outsider with people with whom he would wish to be an insider. With others, it may be different. I have heard of a young midshipman who was made an outsider because he read his Bible morning and evening; and because he would not get drunk when the rest did. A man would be made an outsider in certain parts of this empire, unless he helped to screen the sneaking, cowardly murderer who shoots his landlord from shelter of a tree, because asked to pay his rent. And there are parts of America in which you would become an outsider unless you spoke in praise of the biggest and blackest outrage on humanity that the sun looks down on — I mean negro slavery. Of course, among thieves you must say nothing against stealing, or they might turn you out. But in the main, in this country, people are put outside because it serves them rightly. And the punishment is a fearfully severe one, reaching to sins and to people not otherwise easily punished. You have known persons obliged, by this moral outlawry, to go away from the district or the country where all their interests lay; even great wealth and rank have not sufficed to prevent a man's feeling bitterly that he was made an outsider. You may have seen the fair mansion and the noble trees which their owner could never enjoy, because he durst not show his face where he was known. There was once a man of no small position, who was master of a pack of fox-hounds, let us say in Ethiopia. On a certain Sunday, that man chose to amuse himself by taking out his hounds, and chasing a fox which he had caught, — having cut off the poor fox's feet previously to turning it out to be chased. Of course the brute

(I mean the master of hounds) was brought before the magistrates of that part of Ethiopia, and heavily fined. The law could do no more; and the punishment was most insufficient. The brute probably cared very little for that. But he probably cared a good deal when in a day or two he received a communication from all the princes and nobles of that district, in which they told him that they withdrew from his hunt and cut his acquaintance. Prompt and resolute outsiding inflicted justice in the most satisfactory way.

I have more to say of moral outsiders; but at this point I cannot help looking round, and thinking what a blessing it sometimes is to be physically outside. Not far away, there lies the great city. Inside it the writer lives; and he judges it the best of cities; but now he is beyond it; he is an outsider for three days of perfect rest in the quiet country. It is often worth while to go in, that you may fully appreciate the blessing of coming out. Did you ever, reader, live in July, on that most beautiful Frith of Clyde? After a week in that pure air, and amid that scenery that combines so wonderfully richness and magnificence, you cease fully to understand what a privilege you are enjoying. But go up for a day to the hot, choky Glasgow of July! Remain for five hours in that sweltering atmosphere, hurrying from place to place on business, and stunned by the ceaseless whirl of that hearty and energetic town; and then go back to the seaside! Oh, how delightful to get away into the clear air and the quiet again! And in this green place, I think of the city already spoken of; and of much work and worry there; and feel that here for a little one is outside it all. I think of a certain Gothic building, in which is now sitting an ecclesiastic council which I much revere. I think of the hot atmosphere, of the buzz, of the excitement, of the speeches so very interesting and so very long. I observe from the newspaper that yesterday two gentlemen spoke four hours each. And then I look at that rich sycamore, with foliage so thick, and at the hawthorn blossoms, and at the yellow broom, and at the green grass (for there is "much grass in this place"), and thank God for all!

Last night, on the little village green, I saw several moral outsiders, — I mean members of a class from which respectable folk would for the most part shrink away. There were four poor fellows, acrobats or tumblers; and a girl who is a rope-dancer. They had sent in advance a large bill, which was stuck on a tree, to say there was a grand entertainment coming. The entertainment hardly came up to its description. Still the men did many really wonderful gymnastic feats. They had a striking scene in which to display their ability. It was a beautiful twilight; the little green had fine large trees round it; in the distance there was a great purple hill, and close by was the gray old chapel. The only drawback was a very cold wind. There was a large assemblage of country folk, not very hearty or appreciative spectators; and all evidently regarding themselves as on a totally different level from the poor wanderers. The four men turned somersaults and the like; the poor girl, in her sorry finery, stood by, wrapped in a large shawl till the time of her performance should come. I observed that when the hat went round, the rustic audience evinced great economy in their gifts. The Fool, poor fellow, his face bedaubed with coarse red and white, and wearing a cap with two ears, simulated great spirits, and made many jokes. I looked at him with great pity, and wondered if any human being ever deliberately chooses that way of earning his bread, or whether some men are gradually hedged up to it, without having had a chance of anything else. I was specially sorry for the poor girl, standing with the cold wind blowing through her thin dress. The rustics roared with laughter, as the fool quoted Shakspeare. He was evidently a man of better education than the rest. His most effective point was when he took up a small looking-glass, which was to be given as a prize in some way I did not make out, and, looking into the glass, exclaimed, "Ah, that face! that fine old face! He was a man, take him for all in all," — and so forth. Not since I was a child have I seen such people; and I was greatly touched by the sight of them, and by thinking what kind of life they must lead. I wondered if they ever went to church, or if any clergyman cared for them when they might be sick or dying. And if I had been able, I should assuredly, in defiance of all the laws of Political Economy, have seized them, and taken them away from their sorry occupation, and set them to respectable work, and made them go regularly to church; and, in short, brought them inside.

There is a curious feeling of the difference of being inside and outside, when you are sitting in the cabin of a ship at sea. It is so, even if you be making a voyage no longer than that from Glasgow to Liverpool. It is more so, if you be sailing on distant seas. Fancy a snug little sleeping-cabin, and you lying there in a comfortable berth placed against the side of the ship. You lazily lay your head upon the end of the pillow next the ship's side; about six inches distant from you, but outside, there is a huge shark rubbing its nose against the vessel. Your head and the horrible head of the strange monster are but a few inches apart; happily you are inside and the monster outside. Somehow it seems as if it were a more remarkable thing for a homely Scot, who went in his youth to a Scotch parish school and a Scotch parish church, to be eaten by a shark in a far-away place, than it would be for almost any other human being to meet a like end. The parish school and the Shorter Catechism are things wholly inconsistent with a man's living any other than a decent life, or meeting any other than a quiet Christian close. You know how pleasant and refreshing it is, when you are walking along a dusty road in June, outside some beautiful park, to come to a spot whence you have a view into a green recess of the woods within. And probably you know a city where, as you walk the glaring summer streets, you can look in many places through iron rails into depths of cool grass and verdant leaves that gladden eyes and heart together. And if you pay a yearly subsidy for a share in such a place, you know that when the iron gate swings noisily into its place behind you, and you pass from the pavement to the neat gravelled walk or the cool turf, though it be but for a quarter of an hour at the close of a busy afternoon, you have felt that there is far more than a physical difference between the outside and the inside; you have felt that breaths of balmy country air come back to you, and the remembrance of pleasant country cares. There are human beings, the possessors of fair domains, who seek by lofty walls to keep their fellow-creatures outside their belongings, — even to prevent their fellow-creatures from refreshing their weary eyes by looking upon green expanses which they are not likely to tread. It is a narrow and unworthy mind that feels it cannot fully enjoy its own possessions, unless all mankind be kept definitively outside them! But it testifies to a truly noble nature, when we see what may be seen in many places now: the possessor of a beautiful stretch of landscape around his dwelling cordially welcoming his humbler neighbors to its paths and glades, — giving up the prettiest portion of his park for a cricket-ground for the lads of the adjoining village, — and judging that his charming acres look all the more charming when they cease to be a charming solitude, and are lighted up by happy faces. But a sweet country place is usually in the midst of a sweet country; and there is no place where you value green grass and green trees so much, as when you see them in contrast to the streets of a town, and especially to the ugliest streets of a town. I know a spot which, on a summer day, is peculiarly stifling and dusty, — the dust being mainly the dust of coal. There is a suburban railway station; there are various mills; there are houses of unattractive exterior; everything is glaring in the sunshine; everything is covered with dust. But you enter by a door in a lofty wall, and you feel the difference between being outside and inside. There is a curious, old-fashioned house, surrounded by a pretty garden, laid out with much taste. Everything is green, fresh, cool, quiet. It would be a pleasant spot anywhere; but being where it is, it is a true feast to the eyes. You enjoy the inside so much more keenly, for the contrast with the outside. Green grass, green trees, clear water, abundant flowers and blossoms, freshness and fragrance in the air. And outside, the coal-dust, the glaring pavements, the railway station!

I suppose most people like to contrast insides and outsides, that they may relish one or other the more. Did you ever, my reader, sit in your warm, cheerful library, on a cold winter night, away in the country, which in winter (it must be confessed) looks dreadfully bleak to people accustomed to the town? Your curtains are drawn, and your lamp is lit; and there are your familiar books all round, with their friendly-looking backs. There is the blazing fire, and notwithstanding the condemnation of a certain great Bishop, you do not think it wrong to possess various easy-chairs. All this is pleasant. There is an air of snugness and comfort, and you feel very thankful, it is to be hoped, to the Giver of all. But you do not know, from the survey of the mere interior, how pleasant it is. Go away out, and look at the cold wall outside your chamber. There it is, dark with the plashes of rain, which the howling blast bitterly beats against it. There are the leafless trees, shivering in the blast. There is the stormy sky, with the racking clouds, which the chilly moon is wading through. If you try to make out the landscape as a whole, there is nothing but a dense gloom, with a spectral shape here and there, which you know to be a gate or a tree. On a moonless night, the country is terribly dark. It is dark to a degree that townfolk, with their abundant street lamps, have no idea of. After beholding all these things outside, come in again, and you will understand in some measure how well off you are. You will know the distance there may be, between the two sides of a not very thick wall.

Less than a wall may make the distance. You have probably travelled in a railway carriage through a dark stormy night. If you are a quiet, stay-at-home person, who do not travel so much that all railway travelling has come to be a mere weariness to you, you will enjoy such a night with considerable freshness of interest. And especially, you will feel the distance between being outside and being inside. Inside, the thick cushions; the two great powerful lamps, which give abundant light; the warm rugs and wraps; the hot water stool for your feet; the newspapers, and the new magazine; one or two pleasant companions, who do not trouble you by talking, except at the stations; — the stations forty miles apart. There you lie in luxury, with the feeling that you may honestly do nothing, — that you may rest. And looking through the window, there is the bleak, dark landscape, with all kinds of strange shapes which you cannot make out: the glare cast upon cuttings through which you tear, the fearful hissing and snorting of a passing engine, the row of lighted windows of a passing train; the lurid flame of distant furnaces, the lights of sleeping towns. Yes, a night's travelling between Edinburgh and London is as wonderful a thing as anything recorded in the "Arabian Nights" if it were not that it has grown so cheap and common!

Looking out of the carriage-window over the tracts on either side, and thinking how little parts you from them, you may call to mind a certain ghastly journey by a night-train. A deliberate and cruel murderer, who had committed (it was believed) more than one or two murders for gain, was very justly sentenced to be hanged. He was tried and sentenced in London; and then he was conveyed in a railway carriage a journey of a hundred and forty miles to the place of execution. He sat, manacled, between two officers of justice, through these hours of travelling. It must have been an extraordinary journey! It was a near glimpse of freedom for a man to have when the tightest meshes of the law had grasped him. There he was, inside, — a person going to a dreadful death; and outside, stretching away and away, the free fields; and only the two or three inches between that inside and that outside! I can imagine how the poor wretch thought, Oh, if I could but get into the middle of that thick wood; if I could but hide under that ivied bridge; if I could but put a hundred yards of midnight darkness between me and those terrible keepers who have me in their charge! I can imagine how, as he felt rapid mile after mile bringing him nearer the scaffold, he would wish for some terrible accident, some awful smash; nothing could come amiss to him; nothing could make *him* worse! But in such a case, of course, the little partition between the inside and the outside, — the couple of inches of timber and cloth, the eighth of an inch of glass, — was the little indication of an awful gulf, that had been making for months and perhaps years. Sometimes, indeed, the grievous moral lapse that puts a man in the cage of which he can never get out, — or that puts him outside the pale through which he can never afterwards get in, — may be the doing of a very short time. The hasty blow, the terribly wrong turning, may have marked a change as definite as that when the poor castaway is swept from the ship's deck into the waves of the Atlantic.

In old days, when society was unsettled, it seems as if one would have felt, more vividly than now, the difference between being inside and being outside, in the matter of safety. There must have been a pleasant feeling of security in looking over the battlements of a great castle, and thinking that you were safe inside them. The sense of danger with which men must in those days have gone abroad, would be compensated by the special enjoyment of safety when they were fairly inside some place of strength. Human nature is so made that even though you are aware that no one desires to attack or injure you, still there is a pleasure in thinking, that even if any one had such a desire, he could not. You know how children like to imagine some outer danger, that they may enjoy the sense of safety inside. It is with real delight that your little boy, sitting on your knee, suddenly hides his face in your breast, exclaiming loudly that there is a great bear coming to eat him. He feigns a danger outside, that he may enjoy the feeling of being safe from it. So you will find a man who has been laboring hard, going away for a little rest to some remote quiet place. He tells you, no one can get at him there. The truth is, nobody wants to get at him; but like the child with the great bear, he calls up some vague picture of a great number of people coming to worry him about a great many matters, that he may have the pleasant feeling that he is safe from them where he is. You can think of a man who has committed some crime, flying from justice; and as he puts mile after mile of desolate country between him and the place from which he has fled, thinking that surely he is safe in this retreat. You can think of the forger, a few years since, who fled across the Atlantic; fled from the American seaboard and penetrated deeper and deeper into the backwoods, till he stopped in an utter solitude somewhere in the Far West. You can think how, as week after week went on, he began to feel as if he might breathe in peace at last; and think of the poor wretch, sitting one evening in his little log-house, when two London detectives walked in, having tracked him all this way!

Did you ever see a foolish duck dive at a hole made in the ice; and come up again under the ice at a hopeless distance from the opening? It is a sad thing to see even that poor creature perishing, with only an inch or two of transparent ice between it and the air. You hasten to break a hole near it to let it escape; but by the time the hole is made, the duck is twenty yards off. The duck I have seen; but it must be a fearful case when a human being gets into the like position. You may have lately read how a man was at the bottom of a deep well, when the earth near the top fell together and shut him in. There were ready hands to rescue him; and he was not so shut in but that his voice could be heard hurrying his deliverers. He told them that the water was rising; that it was at his knees, at his breast, at his neck; and the workers above were too late to save him. I suppose it is quite ascertained that in those wicked and cruel ages which ignorant people call the good old times, it was not unusual to wall up a nun in a niche of a massive wall, and leave her there to perish. *Vade in pacem*, were the words that sentenced to this doom; which the reader probably knows, mean not *Depart in peace*, but *Go to rest.* Such was the kindly repose provided in those happy days. And another dismal inside is that of which Samuel Rogers tells us the true story; the massive chest of oak in which a poor Italian girl hid herself, which closed with a spring-lock, and never chanced to be opened for fifty years. You can think of the terrible rush of confused misery in the poor creature's heart when she felt herself shut in, and heard the voices that seemed approaching her die away. But half a century after, when the chest was drawn out to the light and its lid was raised, there was no trace in the mouldering bones of the thrilling anguish which had been endured within that little space. It is a miserable story. Yet perhaps it has its moral analogies not less miserable. There are human beings who by some wrong or hasty step have committed themselves like the poor girl that perished, — who have, in a moral sense, been caught, and who can never get out.

Yes; it is a great question, Outside or Inside; and now, my reader, you must let me remember, drawing these desultory thoughts to a close, that the testing question which puts all mankind to right and left, is just the question, in its most solemn significance, which may be set out in that familiar phrase. There is the Christian fold, — there is the outer world; and we are either within the fold of the Good Shepherd of souls, or without it. It is not a question of degree, as it might be if it founded on our own moral character and deservings. It is the question, have we confided ourselves to the Saviour or not; are we right or wrong; are we within or without? And the two great alternatives, we know, are carried out, without shading off between, into the unseen world. We know that there, when some have gone in to the feast, the door is shut; and others may stand without, and find no admission. Let us humbly pray, that He who came to seek and to save that which was lost may find each reader of this page, a lost sheep by nature, a poor wanderer in the outer wilderness, — and draw all with the cords of love within his fold. And let us humbly pray that at the last, we may all, however our earthly paths have varied, find entrance into that Golden City, which has a wall great and high, whose building is of jasper, and which shall exclude all sin and sorrow; through whose gates, though not shut at all by day (and there shall be no night there), "there shall in no wise enter into it anything that defileth;" and where the blessed inhabitants "shall go no more out," but be safe in their Father's house forever!

CHAPTER VII.

GETTING ON.

EVERYBODY is Going On. We are all getting through our little span of daylight. We are spending the time that is allotted to us, at the rate of three hundred and sixty-five days a year. We are all going on through life, somehow, — not very cheerfully, if one may judge by the careworn, anxious faces of most middle-aged people you pass on the street. But some people are not merely Going On; they are also Getting On, — which is a very different thing. All are growing older; a man here and there is also growing bigger. I mean bigger in a moral sense. As you and I, my reader, look round on those early companions who started with us in the race of life, we can discern that great changes have passed upon many of them. Some who started as cart-horses, of a very shaggy and uncombed appearance, have gradually assumed the aspect of thoroughbred, or at least of well-bred animals. Some who set out as horses sixteen hands high, have shrunk to the size of Shetland ponies. Certain who started as calves, have not attained maturity with advancing years; and instead of turning into consolidated oxen, they have only grown into enormous calves. But without going into such matters, I am sure you know that among your old companions there are those who are shooting ahead of the rest, or who have already shot ahead of them. There are those who are pointed at as Rising Men. They are decidedly Getting On. I do not mean that they are becoming famous, or that they are becoming great men. They have not had much chance of *that.* Their lot has circumscribed their ambition. Their hearts do not beat high for praise; but have known various perplexities as to the more substantial question of the earning of bread and butter. But they are quietly and surely progressing. They have now advanced a good deal beyond what they were five or ten years since. Every profession has its rising men. The Church, the Law, Medicine, Commerce, Literature, have their men who are Getting On, — year by year Getting On. A great many men find their level rather early in life; and remain for many years much the same in standing. They are not growing richer, as they grow older. They are not coming to be better known. They are not gaining a greater place and estimation in their walk of life. Many a little shop-keeper at fifty-five is in worldly wealth much as he was at thirty-five. He has managed to rub on, sometimes with a hard struggle; it has been just enough to make the day provide for the day's wants; and there has been no accumulation of money. Many a domestic servant, after many years of toil, is not a whit better off than when she was a hopeful girl. If she has been provident and self-denying, she may have a few pounds in the Savings'-bank. Many a laboring man in the country has been able each week to make the hard-earned shillings provide food and clothing for his children and their mother; but he has laid up no store; he has not advanced; he lives in the same little cottage; and his poor sticks of furniture are all the worse for their wear; and his carefully-kept Sunday suit is not so trim now as it used to be when he courted his hard-featured wife in her fresh girlhood, and was esteemed as a rustic beau. Many a faithful clergyman at sixty is a poorer man than he was at thirty; or in any case not richer. It has cost many an anxious thought, through these years, to make the ends meet; and that hard task will cost its anxious thoughts to the end. You who wish to have an efficient clergy, who will do their work heartily and well, agitate against that wicked and idiotic notion, that a clergyman is likely to do his work best, if he be crushed down by the pressure of poverty; if his wife be worn into her grave by sorry schemings to make the little means go their farthest; and if his poor little children have to run about without shoes and stockings. There are certain opinions which I should not think of meeting by argument; but rather by the severest application of the cat of ninetails. And one of these is the opinion of the old fool (he was a Scotch Judge) who said that "a puir church would be a pure church."

But returning from this digression, let me repeat, that however hard it may be to explain how some men get on while others do not, there can be no question as to the fact that some men do get on while others do not. People get on in many ways; as you will understand, if you look back a few years, and compare what some of your friends were a few years since with what they are now. There is A, whom you remember in his early days at college, an ungainly cub with a shock head of red hair and a tremendous Scotch accent. That man has taken on polish; he has got on; he has seen the world; he is an accomplished gentleman. There is B, ten years since a poor curate; now risen to the charge of an important parish. There is C; he has married a rich wife; he has a fine house; he has several horses, various dogs, and many pigs; he has made so great a rise in life, that you would say that sometimes when he comes down-stairs in the morning, he must think that he is the wrong man. There is D; some years ago he tried in vain for a certain very small appointment; the other day he was offered one of the most valuable in the same profession, and declined it. There is E; he tried to write for the magazines. His early articles were ignominiously rejected. The other day he got a thousand pounds for one edition of a few of the rejected articles. You know how, in running the race of life, some one individual shows his head a little in front, gradually increases his lead, and finally distances all competition. Once upon a time, there was a staff of newspaper reporters attached to a certain London journal. One of them, not apparently cleverer than the rest, drew bit by bit ahead, till he reached the wool-sack. And when he presided in the great assembly whose speeches he was wont to report, he must unquestionably have felt that he had Got On. Indeed, I have heard that homely phrase applied to him by an old Scotch lady who knew him in his youth; and so who could never speak of his success in life save in modified terms. "Our minister," said the old lady to me, "had two sons. One went to India. As for John, he went to London; and he got on very well." No doubt John had got on; for he was at that time Chief Justice of England. If you look at "The Reliques of Father Prout," you will find a large picture, containing portraits of the contributors to a well-known London magazine, thirty years ago. There is a portrait of a comparatively unnoted man, with a glass stuck in his eye. He was an outsider then; and had given little sign of what he was to be to-day. The portrait is of Mr. Thackeray. You may have heard the name before. This very day, I was told about a man who forty years since opened a little shop, stocked chiefly with coarse towels. So my informant averred. If so, the demand for coarse towels in a certain great town must have been enormous, or the individual in question must have been most fortunate in drawing general attention to his coarse towels; for he drew ahead of other dealers in towels, and became one of the greatest merchant-princes of England. But without taking extreme cases, you know that within more modest limits, there are people who are steadily Getting On. While one man lives for thirty years in the same house, and maintains the same general appearance; his next neighbor ascends the scale of fashion; gets time after time a better house, till he attains a grand country mansion; and from the total absence of any save the conveyance common to mankind, attains to the phaeton, the brougham, and the family chariot. One preacher does his duty steadily and respectably, year after year; and no one thinks anything particular about him. Another tears like a rocket to the highest elevation of the preacher's precarious popularity. His church-doors are mobbed; his fame overspreads the land; his portrait is in the shop-windows; his sermons sell by scores of thousands.

How is it that men Get On? How is it that in every walk of life, there are those who draw ahead of their competitors? It is a very simple and primary notion, not likely to be entertained unless by youthful and unsophisticated minds in remote rural districts, that the most deserving men Get On the best. To gain any advantage or eminence, indeed, which is not bestowed by high-handed patronage, a man must have a certain amount of merit. The horse that wins the Derby must unquestionably be able to gallop at a very great pace. Of course, if the Derby prize were given by patronage, it might occasionally fall to a horse with only three legs. And there are places in the Church and the Law which are filled up by unchecked patronage; and in which a perfectly analogous state of matters may be discerned. It would be insulting some men to suggest that they were placed where they are because they were the best men eligible; or even because they were fit to be placed there at all. You may have known instances in which a man was put in a certain place, because he was the worst man, or one of the worst men, that could be found. But even in cases where the eminence is not arbitrarily given, — where it is understood to be earned by the man himself, and not allotted to him by some other man, — it is a simple and unsophisticated notion, that the best man gets the best place. The winner of the Derby must be able to gallop very fast; but nine times out of ten, he is by no means the best horse that starts. A bad place at starting; an unlucky push from a rival in mid career; the awkward straining of a muscle; a little nervousness or want of judgment in the jockey who rides him; and the best horse is beaten by a very inferior one, more lucky or better handled. I am obliged to say, as the result of all my observation of the way in which human beings Get On, that human beings get on mainly by Chance, or Luck. I use the words in their ordinary meaning. I mean that human beings Get On or fail to Get On, in a fashion that looks fortuitous. There must be merit, in walks where men have to make their own way; but that a man may get on, he must be seconded by Good Luck, or at least not crossed by Ill Luck. We must speak of things, you know, as they appear to our ignorance. I know there is a Higher Hand; and I humbly recognize *that*. I know that "Promotion cometh neither from the East, nor from the West, nor from the South; but God is the Judge; he putteth down one, and setteth up another." We all feel that. I believe that these words of the Psalmist give us the entire philosophy of Getting On. It is a matter of God's sovereignty; and God's sovereignty, as it affects human beings, we speak of as their Good or Ill Luck. Of course, there is no chance in the matter; everything is tightly arranged and governed; and doubtless, if we could see aright, we should see that there are wise and good reasons for all; but as we do not know the reasons, and as we cannot foresee the arrangement, we fall back on a word which expresses our ignorance; and which states the fact of the apparent arbitrariness of the government of Providence. Nothing can be more certain than the fact, that there are men who are lucky; and other men who are unlucky. The unlucky, perhaps, need it all;

and the lucky can stand it all; but there is the fact. And we know that there are blessed compensations, not known to onlookers, which may make the thorn in the flesh or the crook in the lot a true blessing; which cause men thankfully to say that it was good for them that they were afflicted and disappointed; good for them that they did not Get On. The wise man Jabez, you remember, knew that God might "bless indeed," while to other eyes He did not seem to bless at all. And so his prayer was, not that he might absolutely Get On; but that he might Get On or fail to do so as God saw best. "Oh, that thou wouldst bless me *indeed!*" And so, speaking in ordinary language, let me say that I hold by the Psalmist. It is God's sovereignty. *Fiat Voluntas Tua!* The thing that makes men Get On in this world, is mainly their luck; and in a very subordinate degree, their merit or desert.

Life is a lottery. No doubt there is no real chance in life; but then there is no real chance in any lottery. I do not hesitate to say that what we deserve has very little to do with our Getting On. And all human scheming and labor have very little to do with the actual result in Getting On. And for this reason, I find a great defect in all that I have seen written as to the arts of self-advancement, whether these arts be honest and commendable, or otherwise. It is easy to point out a number of honorable means which tend to help a man on, and a number of contemptible tricks and dodges which tend towards worldly wealth and influence. But the practical use of all these directions is nullified by the fact, that some fortuitous accident may come across all the hard work and self-denial of the worthy man, or all the dirty trickery of the diplomatic cheat; and make all perfectly futile. Honest industry and perseverance, also resolute selfishness, meanness, toadyism, and roguery, tend to various forms of worldly success. But you can draw no assurance from these general principles, as to what either may do for yourself. Out of a hundred men, the Insurance tables will tell you very nearly how many will live for five or ten years to come; but not the slightest assurance can be conveyed by these tables to any individual man of the hundred as to his expectations of life. I have a practical lesson to draw from all this, by and by; but here let it be repeated, that as a general rule, it is not the most deserving who Get On, but the most lucky. My reader, if you have met success in life yourself, you know this well. The man who has succeeded knows this far better than the man who has failed. The writer states his principle the more confidently, because he knows he has himself got on infinitely better than he deserves. He looks back on the ruck with which he started, and he sees that he has drawn ahead of some who deserved at least as well; who deserved far better. The writer says earnestly that it is not the most deserving who get on the best; not because he thinks he has got less than he deserves, but because he knows he has got an immense deal more. For these things he knows Whom to thank; and he desires to be thankful.

Chance, then (which means God's Providence), advances people in many ways. A man publishes a book. It meets great success. There is no particular reason. Other books as good, and some books a great deal better, prove entire failures. A man goes to the bar, and shortly a stream of briefs begins to set in towards his chambers. Men of equal ability, and eager to excel in their profession, wait wearily on year after year. A man goes into the Church; he is put in conspicuous places, where his light is not hid under a bushel; he gets large preferments, no one can exactly say why. He fills respectably the place where he is put; but doubtless there are many who would fill it just as well. You will find a man chance upon a general reputation for great learning, of which he never gave the slightest proof. Somehow it became the fashion to speak of him as the possessor of unexplored mines of information. Then you know how a man then and there becomes a privileged person, you cannot say how. A privileged person means a man who is permitted to say and do the silliest and most insolent things, and to evince the most babyish pettedness of temper, — things for which anybody else would be kicked, or esteemed as an idiot; but when the privileged man does all this, every one sets himself to smooth the creature down if he be petted, and to applaud his silly jokes if he be jocular. I do not know any more signal instance of the arbitrary allotment of things in this world, than this. It has been truly said that one man may steal a horse, while another must not look over the gate. To a certain extent, it is a matter of natural constitution. You remember how the dog was accustomed, without rebuke, to jump upon his master's knee; while the donkey was chastised severely on endeavoring to do the same thing. You will find a man who is always being stroked down and flattered by the members of some public body, to which he never rendered any particular service. One can understand why the great Duke of Wellington, even when he had grown an extreme obstruction to army business and reform, should be deferred to by the nation for which he had done so much; but you may have known people treated with the like deference, who had never done anything through life but diligently aim at securing the greatest advantage of the greatest number; which (it is well known) is Number One. Then there are men who Get On, even to places of very great dignity, because somehow they have got into the track, and are pushed on with very little motive force of their own. It would be invidious to mention striking instances of this: but it would be very easy. Other men Get On, by being appointed, with little competition, to some position which at the time is not worth much, but which grows important and valuable. And a worthier way of Getting On, is when a man, by his doings and character, makes a position important, which in other hands would not be so.

The Chance (as already explained) which rules events in this life, never appears more decidedly than in making the diligent efforts of some men successful, and of other men futile. We can see the arts which men use, thinking to advance themselves; and no doubt these arts often tend directly to that end; but then Chance comes in to say whether these arts shall signally fail or splendidly succeed. I have known a laborious student get up many pages of Greek for an examination; all his pages most thoroughly, save two or three which were hastily read over. And upon the examination-day, sure enough he was taken upon the pages he did not know well, while his competitor was taken on his pet page, which he knew by heart. And there were scores of pages which that competitor had never looked at, but he trusted his Luck, and it did not fail him.

It may be assumed as certain, that all men would like to Get On. If you see a number of cabs upon a stand, you may be quite sure that any one of them would take a fare if it could get it. And a man, in all ordinary cases, by entering any profession, becomes as a cab upon the stand waiting for a fare. If he stand idle in the market-place all day, it may be taken for granted that it is because no man has hired him.

And though we may have quite outgrown our early ambitions; though we may never have had much ambition; though we may be quite contented with our present position and circumstances; still, we should all like to Get On. We do not talk of ambition, in the case of commonplace folk like ourselves; and though the "love of fame" has been called the "universal passion," I believe that it is practically confined to a very little fraction of mankind. We call it ambition when Mr. Disraeli goes in for leader of the House of Commons; or when Napoleon twists his way to a throne. We do not call it ambition when a clergyman would like a larger congregation to preach to, or another hundred or two a year of income. We do not speak of ambition in such cases; it is only that people would like to Get On a little. We like to think that we are Getting On; that we live in a better house than we used to do; that our little library is gradually growing; that our worldly means are improving; that we are a little wiser and better than we used to be. But though we may take for granted, that all men would like to Get On, we may be assured that there are many who would not take much trouble to do so. Their wishes are moderate; they have learned to be content. They will not fret themselves into a fever; they will not push. And much less will they sneak, or cheat, or wriggle. If success comes, they are pleased; but they are not vexed though it do not come. They look with interest, and with some amusement, at the diplomatic schemes of their friends, who enter themselves in the race of ambition. They see that pertinacious pushing will make a man Get On, unless he be very unlucky or very incapable. But they do not think it worth while pertinaciously to push. They see that judicious puffing, on your own part and that of your friends, is a helpful thing; but they shrink from puffing themselves, or from hearing their friends puff them. Puffing is a great power; as Mr. Barnum and others know. It is a great thing, to have friends to back you and puff you. One man publishes a book. He does not know a soul who ever printed a line. There is not a human being to say a good word of his book for friendship's sake. Another author has a host of literary friends; and when his book comes out, they raise a *sough* of applause through the press. And all this is very natural; and is not unfair. Only the unlucky man who has got no friends will probably grumble. Yet all this will not always succeed. I have known two books come out together. One was written by a man who had no writing friends; the other by a man who had many. The former was reviewed widely and favorably; the other was very little noticed by the reviewers. But you cannot always force things upon the reading public. The unreviewed book sold splendidly; the other hardly sold at all. The unreviewed book enriched its author; the other slightly impoverished its author. All this, of course, was Luck again.

I have already stated what appears to me the great defect in all treatises on the arts of self-advancement and self-help. There appears to me a fallacy at the foundation of all their instructions. They all say, in one form or other, "Do so and so, and you will Get On." Some of these treatises recommend fair and worthy means; as industry, self-denial, perseverance, honesty, and the like. Others of them recommend unworthy means; as selfishness, unscrupulousness, impudence, toadyism, sneakiness, and the like. But they fail to allow for Chance or Providence. They fail to bring out the utter uncertainty which attends all arts for Getting On. No mortal can say how a man is to Get On. A poor Scotch lad, walking the London streets, fell into a cellar and broke his leg. *That* made his fortune. The wealthy owner of the cellar took him up, and pushed him on; and he rose to be Lord Mayor of London and an eminent member of Parliament. A certain man (and a good man too) became a Bishop through accidentally attracting the notice of a disreputable peeress who was in high favor with a disreputable monarch, who once reigned (let us say) in the centre of Africa. The likeliest arts, whether honest or dishonest, may fail utterly. And the lesson, I think, is this: Do your duty quietly and honestly; Don't push, don't puff; Don't set your heart upon any worldly end; it is not worth while; if success comes, well; if it does not come, you do not mind much. "Seekest thou great things for thyself? seek them not!" There never were words written more worthy of being remembered and acted on by all men. There is no use in being ambitious. Being ambitious just means setting your whole heart on Getting On; and in this world people seldom get the thing on which they set their heart. And no matter how you may labor to attain your end, you cannot make sure of attaining it. You may probably see it carried away by some easy-going man who cared very little for it, and took very little trouble to get it. Read Mr. Smiles' excellent book on "Self-Help." It will do you good to read it. It will spur you to do your best, to see what other men have done. But remember, you are in God's hands. The issue is with Him. It no more follows that if you work like George Stephenson or Lord Eldon, you will get on as they did; than that if you eat the same thing for breakfast as the man who gets the great prize in a lottery, you will get the prize like him. Still, Mr. Smiles will do you good. Unless luck sets very greatly against you, you may, by honestly doing your best, Get On fairly. Your chance of Getting On to the highest point of success is just about the same as your chance of being smashed altogether. It is not great. And remember, my friend, that it is not worldly success that is the best thing we can get in this world. There is something far better. And perhaps it may be by forbidding that you should Get On, that God may discipline you into *that*. I should feel very great interest in reading the lives of a number of men who honestly did their best, and failed; yet who were not soured by failure; men who, like St. Paul, bore the painful weight through life, and bore it kindly and humbly; getting great good and blessing out of it all. Let us always keep it in our remembrance, that there is something far better than any amount of worldly success, which may come of worldly failure.

Still, remembering all this, it is interesting to look at the various arts and devices by which men have Got On. Judicious puffing is a great thing. But it must be very judicious. Some people irritate one by their constant stories as to their own great doings. I have known people who had really done considerable things; yet who did not get the credit they deserved, just because they were given to vaporing of what they had done. It is much better to have friends and relatives to puff you; to record what a splendid fellow you are, and what wonderful events have befallen you. Even here, if you become known as one of a set who puff each other, your laudations will do harm instead of good. It is a grand thing to have relations and friends who have the power to actually confer material success. Who would not wish to be Dowb, that so he might be "taken care of?" You have known men at the Bar, to whom some powerful relative gave a tremendous lift at starting in their profession. Of course this would in some cases only make their failure more apparent, unless they were really equal to the work to which they were set. There is a cry against Nepotism. It will not be shared in by the *Nepotes*. It must be a fine thing to be one of them. Unhappily, they must always be a very small minority; and thus the cry against them will be the voice of a great majority. I cannot but observe that the names of men who hold canonries at cathedrals, and other valuable preferments in the Church, are frequently the same as the name of the Bishop of the diocese. I do not complain of that. It is the plain intention of Providence that the children should suffer for their fathers' sins, and gain by their fathers' rise. It is utterly impossible to start all human beings for the race of life, on equal terms. It is utterly impossible to bring all men up to a rope stretched across the course, and make all start fair. If a man be a drunken blackguard, or a heartless fool, his children *must* suffer for it; *must* start at a disadvantage. No human power can prevent *that*. And on the other hand, if a man be industrious and able, and rise to great eminence, his children gain by all this. Robert Stephenson had a splendid start, because old George his father got on so nobly. Lord Stanley entered political life at an immense advantage, because he was Lord Derby's son. And if any reader of this page had some valuable office to give away, and had a son, brother, or nephew, who deserved it as well as anybody else, and who he could easily think deserved it a great deal better than anybody else, I have little doubt that the reader would give that valuable office to the son, brother, or nephew. I have known, indeed, magnanimous men who acted otherwise, who in exercising abundant patronage suffered no nepotism; it was a positive disadvantage to be related to these men; they would not give their relatives ordinary justice. The fact of your being connected with them made it tolerably sure that you would never get anything they had to give. All honor to such men! Yet they surpass average humanity so far, that I do not severely blame those who act on lower motives. I do not find much fault with a certain Bishop who taught me theology in my youth, because I see that he has made his son a canon in his cathedral. I notice, without indignation, that the individual who holds the easy and lucrative office of Associate in certain Courts of Law, bears the same name with the Chief Justice. You have heard how Lord Ellenborough was once out riding on horseback, when word was brought him of the death of a man who held a sinecure office with a revenue of some thousands a year. Lord Ellenborough had the right of appointment to that office. He instantly resolved to appoint his son. But the thought struck him, that he might die before reaching home, — he might fall from his horse; or the like. And so the eminent Judge took from his pocket a piece of paper and a pencil, and then and there wrote upon his saddle a formal appointment of his son to that wealthy place. And as it was a place which notoriously was to be given, not to a man who should deserve it, but merely to a man who might be lucky enough to get it, I do not know that Lord Ellenborough deserved to be greatly blamed. In any case, his son, as he quarterly pocketed the large payment for doing nothing, would doubtless hold the blame of mankind as of very little account.

But whether you Get On by having friends who cry you up, or by having friends who can materially advance you, of course it is your luck to have such friends. We all know that it is "the accident of an accident" that makes a man succeed to a peerage or an estate. And though trumpeting be a great fact and power, still your luck comes in to say whether the trumpet shall in your case be successful. One man, by judicious puffing, gets a great name; another, equally deserving, and apparently in exactly the same circumstances, fails to get it. No doubt the dog who gets an ill name, even if he deserves the ill name, deserves it no more than various other sad dogs who pass scot free. Over all events, all means and ends in this world, there rules God's inscrutable sovereignty. And to our view, that direction appears quite arbitrary. "One shall be taken, and the other left." "Jacob have I loved and Esau have I hated." "Hath not the potter power over the clay, of the same lump to make one vessel unto honor, and another unto dishonor?" A sarcastic London periodical lately declared that the way to attain eminence in a certain walk of life, was to "combine mediocrity of talent with family affliction." And it is possible that instances might be indicated in which that combination led to very considerable position. But there are many more cases in which the two things coexisted in a very high degree, without leading to any advancement whatsoever. It is all luck again.

A way in which small men sometimes Get On, is by finding ways to be helpful to bigger men. Those bigger men have occasional opportunities of helping those who have been helpful to them. If you yourself, or some near relation of yours, yield effectual support to a candidate at a keenly-contested county election, you may possibly be repaid by influence in your favor brought to bear upon the Government of the day. From a bishopric down to a beadleship, I have known such means serve valuable ends. It is a great thing to have any link, however humble, and however remote, that connects you with a Secretary of State, or any member of the Administration. Political tergiversation is a great thing. Judicious ratting, at a critical period, will generally secure some one considerable reward. In a conservative institution to stand almost alone in professing very liberal opinions; or in a liberal institution to stand almost alone in professing conservative opinions; will probably cause you to Get On. The leaders of parties are likely to reward those who among the faithless are faithful to them; and who hold by them under difficulties. Still, luck comes in here. While some will attain great rewards by professing opinions very inconsistent with their position, others by doing the same things merely bring themselves into universal ridicule and contempt. It is a powerful thing, to have abundant impudence; to be quite ready to ask for whatever you want. Worthier men wait till their merits are found out; you don't. You may possibly get what you ask; and then you may snap your fingers in the face of the worthier man. By a skilful dodge, A got something which ought to have come to B. Still, A can drive in dignity past B, covering him with mud from his chariot-wheels. There was a man in the last century who was made a bishop by George III., for having published a poem on the death of George II. That poem declared that George II. was removed by Providence to heaven, because he was too good for this world. You know what kind of man George II. was; you know whether even Bishop Porteus could possibly have thought he was speaking the truth in publishing that most despicable piece of toadyism. Yet Bishop Porteus was really a good man, and died in the odor of sanctity. He was merely a little yielding. Honesty would have stood in the way of his Getting On; and so honesty had to make way for the time. Many people know that a certain Bishop was to have been made Archbishop of Canterbury; but that he threw away his chance by an act of injudicious honesty. On one occasion, he opposed the Court, under very strong conscientious convictions of duty. If he had just sat still, and refrained from bearing testimony to what he held for truth, he would have Got On much farther than he ever did. I am very sure the good man never regretted that he had acted honestly!

Judicious obscurity is often a reason for advancing a man. You know nothing to his prejudice. Eminent men have always some enemies; there are those who will secretly hate them just because they are eminent; and no one can say how or when the most insignificant enemy may have an opportunity to put a spoke in the wheel, and upset the coach in which an eminent man is advancing to what would have crowned his life. While nothing can be more certain than that if you know nothing at all about a man, you know no harm of him. There are many people who will oppose a man seeking for any end, just because they know him. They don't care about a total stranger gaining the thing desired; but they cannot bear that any one they know should reach it. They cannot make up their mind to *that.* You remember a curious fact brought out by Cardinal Wiseman in his "Lives of the Last Four Popes." There are certain European kings who have the right to veto a Pope. Though the choice of the conclave fall on him, these kings can step in and say, No. They are called to give no reason. They merely say, Whoever is to be Pope, it shall not be that man. And the Cardinal shows us, that as surely as any man seems likely to be elected Pope who has ever been Papal Ambassador at the court of any of those kings, so surely does the king at whose court he was veto him! In short, the king is a man; and he cannot bear that any one he knows should be raised to the mystical dignity of the Papacy. But the monarch has no objection to the election of a man whom he knows nothing about. And as the more eminent cardinals are sure to have become known, more or less intimately, to all the kings who have the right to veto, the man elected Pope is generally a very obscure and insignificant Cardinal. Then there is a pleasant feeling of superiority and patronage in advancing a small man, a man smaller than yourself. You may have known men who were a good deal consulted as to the filling up of vacant offices in their own profession, who made it their rule strongly to recommend men whose talent was that of decent mediocrity, and never to mention men of really shining ability. And if you suggest to them the names of two or three persons of very high qualifications, as suitable to fill the vacant place, you will find the most vigorous methods instantly employed to make sure that whoever may be successful, it shall not be one of these. "Oh, *he* would never do!"

It is worth remembering, as further proof, how little you can count on any means certainly conducing to the end of Getting On, that the most opposite courses of conduct have led men to great success. To be the toady of a great man is a familiar art of self-advancement. There once was a person who by doing extremely dirty work for a notorious peer, attained a considerable place in the government of this country. But it is a question of luck, after all. Sometimes it has been the making of a man, to insult a Duke, or to bully a Chief Justice. It made him a popular favorite; it enlisted general sympathy on his side; it gained him credit for nerve and courage. But public feeling, and the feeling of the dispensers of patronage in all walks of life, oscillates so much, that at different times, the most contradictory qualities may commend a man for preferment. You may have known a man who was much favored by those in power, though he was an extremely outspoken, injudicious, and almost reckless person. It is only at rare intervals that such a man finds favor; a grave, steady, and reliable man, who will never say or do anything outrageous, is for the most part preferred. And now and then you may find a highly cultivated congregation, wearied by having had for its minister for many years a remarkably correct and judicious though tiresome preacher, making choice for his successor of a brilliant and startling orator, very deficient in taste and sense. A man's luck, in all these cases, will appear, if it bring him into notice just at the time when his special characteristics are held in most estimation. If for some specific purpose, you desire to have a horse which has only three legs, it is plain that if two horses present themselves for your choice, one with three legs and the other with four, you will select and prefer the animal with three. It will be the best, so far as it concerns you. And its good luck will appear in this: that it has come to your notice just when your liking happened to be a somewhat peculiar one. In like manner, you may find people say, In filling up this place at the present time, we don't want a clever man, or a well-informed man, or an accomplished and presentable man; we want a meek man, a humble man, a man who will take snubbing freely, a rough man, a man like ourselves. And I have known many cases, in which, of several competitors, one was selected just for the possession of qualities which testified his inferiority to the others. But then, in this case, that which was absolutely the worst, was the best for the particular case. The people *wanted* a horse with three legs, and when such an animal presented itself they very naturally preferred him to the other horses which had four legs. The horses with four legs naturally complained of the choice, and thought themselves badly used when the screw was taken in preference. They were wrong. There are places for which a rough man is better than a smooth one; a dirty man than a clean one; in the judgment (that is) of the people who have the filling up of the place. I certainly think their judgment is wrong. But it *is* their judgment, and of course they act upon it.

As regards the attainment of very great and unusual

wealth, by business or the like, it is very plain how much there is of luck. A certain degree of business talent is of course necessary, in the man who rises in a few years from nothing to enormous wealth; but it is Providence that says who shall draw the great prize; for other men with just as much ability and industry entirely fail. Talent and industry in business may make sure, unless in very extraordinary circumstances, of decent success; but Providence fixes who shall make four hundred thousand a year. The race is not to the swift, nor the battle to the strong, nor riches to men of understanding; that is, their riches are not necessarily in proportion to their understanding. Trickery and cheating, not crossed by ill-luck, may gain great wealth. I shall not name several instances which will occur to every one. But I suppose, my friend, that you and I would cut off our right hand before we should Get On in worldly wealth by such means as these. You must make up your mind, however, that you will not be envious when you see the fine house, and the horses and carriages of some successful trickster. All this indeed might have been had; but *you* would not have it at the price. That worldly success is a great deal too dear, which is to be gained only by sullying your integrity! And I gladly believe that I know many men, whom no material bribe would tempt to what is mean or dishonest.

There is something curious in the feeling which many people cherish towards an acquaintance who becomes a successful man. Getting On gives some people mortal offence. To them, success is an unpardonable crime. They absolutely hate the man that Gets On. Timon, you remember, lost the affection of those who knew him, when he was ruined; but depend upon it, there are those who would have hated Timon much worse had he suddenly met some great piece of good fortune. I have already said that these envious and malicious people can better bear the success of a man whom they do not know. They cannot stand it, when an old school-companion shoots ahead. They cannot stand it, when a man in their own profession attains to eminence. They diligently thwart such an one's plans, and then chuckle over their failure, saying, with looks of deadly malice, "Ah, this will do him a great deal of good!"

But now, my reader, I am about to stop. Let me briefly sum up my philosophy of Getting On. It is this: A wise man in this world will not set his heart on Getting On, and will not push very much to Get On. He will do his best, and humbly take with thankfulness what the Hand above sends him. It is not worth while to push. The whole machinery that tends to earthly success, is so capricious and uncertain in its action, that no man can count upon it, and no wise man will. A chance word, a look, the turning of a straw, may make your success or mar it. A man meets you on the street and says, Who is the person for such a place, great or small? You suddenly think of somebody, and say He is your man, and the thing is settled. A hundred poor fellows are disappointed. You did not know about them, or their names did not occur to you. You put your hand into a hat, and drew out a name. You stuck a hook into your memory, and this name came out. And *that* has made the man's fortune. And the upshot of the whole matter is, that such an infinitude of little fortuitous circumstances may either further or prevent our Getting On; the whole game is so complicated, that the right and happy course is humbly to do your duty and leave the issue with God. Let me say it again: "Seekest thou great things for thyself? Seek them not!" It is not worth while. All your seeking will not make you sure of getting them; the only things you will make sure of will be fever and toil and suspense. We shall not push, or scheme, or dodge, for worldly success. We shall succeed exactly as well, and we shall save ourselves much that is wearisome and degrading. Let us trust in God, my friend, and do right; and we shall Get On as much as He thinks good for us. And it is not the greatest thing to Get On. I mean, to Get On in matters that begin and end upon this world. There is a progress in which we are sure of success, if we earnestly aim at it; which is the best Getting On of all. Let us "grow in grace." Let us try by God's aid to grow better, kinder, humbler, more patient, more earnest to do good to all. If the germ of the better life be implanted in us by the Blessed Spirit, and tended by Him day by day; if we trust our Saviour and love our God, then our whole existence, here and hereafter, will be a glorious progress from good to better. We shall always be Getting On!

CHAPTER VIII.

AT THE LAND'S END.

JUST a quarter of an hour ago, an aged man, the most intelligent and pleasant of hostlers, zealous in Methodism, and skilled in the characteristics of horses, said to the present writer, "Stand on that rock." And as he said the words, he pointed to a little flat expanse of granite, three or four feet square. The present writer obeyed. And then the aged and intelligent man added, emphatically and solemnly, "Now, sir, you are standing on THE LAND'S HEND."

When I used continually to read the life of that great and good man, Dr. Arnold, (to whom, and to whose biographer, many thousands of human beings owe some of the most healthful influence that ever went to ameliorate their heart and life,) I remember thinking, a good many times, that one subject in a list of subjects for English verses to be prescribed to the boys of the sixth class, was a most suggestive one. It was, as the intelligent reader has anticipated, *The Land's End.*

One had a vague idea, that a great many fine things were to be said upon that subject. But if I ever thought what they were, I am sorry to say that they have quite vanished from remembrance now. At present, I can only look and feel, in a very confused fashion. For this is the Land's End. Here I am, on the extreme verge of England; this paper is laid on a rough granite rock, in a little recess which keeps off the wind. All this little headland is granite, shattered and splintered as if by lightning. The granite is in many places covered with lichens; and here and there a bright sprig of heather looks out from a little nook in which it has been able to root itself. The sea is roaring eighty feet below. Eighty feet make all the elevation; of course the mere height is very poor when compared with that of many bits of the Scotch coast. The descent to the sea is perpendicular; the sea below is not deep just at this point. Out, a mile and a half from shore, you might see the Longships Rocks; detached islets rising in a line, very sharply out of the sea, and running up almost into spires. On one of them is a light-house. Three men live in it. A few years ago, a young man who had been absent from his family for twelve years, came back to visit his old home hard by. His father was one of the keepers of the light-house, and as it was his turn to take charge of the lights that month, he could not come ashore to see his son till a few days should pass. The morning after the son's arrival, it was too stormy to go out to the light-house to visit his father, and he came to this spot to have as near a view as might be of the place where his father was. He fell over the rocks and was killed. It is a touching story; if you cannot see why, I need not attempt to show you.

Off on the right, at three miles' distance, is a black-looking promontory, called Cape Cornwall. When you visit the place, my reader, the old man will tell you it is the only cape in England. There are heads; there are points; there is a ness; but there is no other cape. You would think that Cape Cornwall reaches into the sea farther than the Land's End itself; but your eye deceives you. It falls short of its more famous neighbor by several hundred yards. Looking down from this recess, you may see a number of rocks, greater and less, rising out of the sea; each with a ring of white foam at its base. Far out, you may just trace the outline of Scilly; for the day is not very clear.

When you come to this spot, my friend, you will have all the sights shown you by that most intelligent old man already mentioned; that is, of course, if he and you are spared to meet. You will see, very near the End, the deep marks of a horse's hoofs in the turf, within two feet of the verge. A stupid and blustering idiot once made a bet that he would ride on horseback to the Land's End; meaning to the very extremity of the little rocky headland. He forced his horse down the steep and rugged descent from the heathery plateau above, and upon the neck of turf-covered rock that joins the headland to the shore. But when the horse reached this slippery neck, he testified how much more sense he had than the blustering idiot who rode him, by refusing to go any farther. The blustering idiot goaded him with whip and spur; and slipping upon the short turf, the poor creature fell; and clung by his fore feet in the marks you see, before making the awful plunge below. The fall was not into water, but upon sharp rocks; and the poor horse miserably perished. I lamented the horse's fate; and I could not but conclude that had his master been smashed instead of himself, the nobler creature of the two would have been saved; and the loss to mankind would have been inappreciably small. It is fifty-five years since the horse's hoofs clung to that last hope; but the deep marks have been diligently kept clear, and they remain as when the horse was wickedly killed; serving as a monument of his sad fate, and of what a brainless fool his master was. After standing on the rocky table which is emphatically styled the HEND, you will clamber down a rough path, and lie down at all your length on a very overhanging crag. Here your head will project much over the sea; and the intelligent old man will keep a tight hold of your feet. And now, looking away to the right, you will discern the reason why you were brought to this precarious position. You will see that the rocky neck joining the End to the shore, is penetrated clear through by a lofty Gothic arch, through which the waves fret in foam. You will be told of another lesser arch, which you cannot see. These have been worn in the lapse of ages; and some day, if the world stands, the superincumbent rock will fall, and the Land's End will become a little rocky islet. You can see many traces in the rocks near, of the like having happened before. Doubtless the Cornwall coast once reached at least as far seaward as those Longships Rocks. And coming up from this spot, you will reach the neck once more; and here the old man (skilful hostler and zealous Methodist), if he thinks you a fit person so to distinguish; if he sees you are a man or a woman who can sympathize with him and understand him; will point with reverence to a square block of granite that looks through the turf; and tell you that a good man whose memory *he* holds very dear, and whose memory can be indifferent to no human being who reverences simple-hearted devotion to the best good of his fellow-creatures, has been before you here. "John Wesley stood on that stone, and made verses of poetry," said the old man to me; and I am glad to say that he then went on, with much simple solemnity, to repeat the verses from end to end. I doubt not you know them. They are the verses in which the good man tells us how, standing physically "between two seas;" standing on this narrow neck with the Atlantic chafing on either hand beneath; he remembered that he, and every human being with him, stands morally and spiritually between two oceans more solemn than that; and prayed humbly that the pilgrimage might end well for all. The writer is a churchman; churchman both by head and by heart; but when he heard again the simple lines (which he confesses struck him as extremely poor when tried by merely æsthetic rules), he could not but stand reverentially on the stone where Wesley's feet had stood; and think of the old man, with his white hair, his kindly face, his warm heart, and his beautifully-starched bands; and heartily ask, in a fashion very familiar to us all, for more of Wesley's single-minded spirit.

And now I have sent the old man away, thanking him very much for the intelligent and interesting way in which he told his story; and I wait here by myself. I have written these lines which you have read, since he departed. At a spot like this, a party of visitors along with you is fatal to your feeling the genius of the place; and after the most intelligent guide has told you all he can tell, it is a relief to get rid of him. I want to feel that I am here. And first, I am aware that I am not disappointed. I went many miles round to-day to see the Logan Rock. The Logan Rock is an imposition. It is a delusion and a snare. You are told it is a mass of granite weighing eighty tons; and that it is so balanced by nature on a pivot of stone, that a touch from the hand can make it rock back and forward. To rock back and forward is apparently an idea conveyed in Cornish speech by the verb *to log;* and the Rock, though its name be spelled as above, is called the *Loggin Rock*, to describe its nature. You drive or walk ten miles from Penzance, by fearfully steep roads the last miles, till you come to a very dirty little village at the top of a hill. I have seldom seen more squalid cottages. I wish I knew the name of the proprietor of the estate on which they are built. A man, who has been lounging about on the road to the village, approaches as you stop at the door of the neat little inn; and the driver of the vehicle which has borne you from Penzance introduces him as your guide. You follow him along a well-defined path, through fields of ripening grain, for about half a mile. Then you come upon a rocky height, from which you discern the sea below you on two sides, within two hundred yards. You can indistinctly trace the outline of the walls of an ancient fortress upon that rocky height. Then you scramble down upon a little isthmus, as at the Land's End; the isthmus spreads into a little headland, made of huge blocks of granite. On either hand below you can see a beach of silvery white sand. As you are scrambling down the descent to the isthmus, you observe a man leisurely walking up the opposite ascent; and you become aware of the extent to which the division of labor is carried in that little Cornish village. One man is your guide to the Rock; his business is to conduct you along a path you could not possibly miss, even without a guide. A second man waits your arrival at the Rock; his business is to give it a push with his shoulder, and set it *loggin.* The Rock is a large mass, which may possibly weigh eighty tons; it certainly does not look as if it did. It lies on the landward slope of the headland which you reach by the isthmus. And when the man puts his shoulder to it, and gives it a push, you may, if you shut one eye, and look very sharply with the other, see the rock move a distance of perhaps one inch; possibly two. Let me strongly advise the reader to spare himself the trouble of going to see that sight.

But sitting on a rock at the Land's End, you will not feel disappointed. The interest here is not the factitious one of seeing a large stone moved an inch or two. It is the interest of looking at a wild piece of rocky coast, round whose name there clusters a crowd of associations. How familiar the name is; how often, when a child, you pointed this place out on the map; how many times you have wondered what it would be like; and wondered if you would ever see it! A quarter of a mile out to sea, just below, there is a black-looking rock; on that rock at this minute there are sitting twelve cormorants. Now and then one of them skims off over the sea. The day has become overcast; there is not a soul near. You cannot help having an eerie kind of feeling. You think it wonderful to find yourself here.

Sitting here, I think of a passage in the works of the most pleasing of English essayists, whom the writer is so happy as to call his friend. You will find the passage in "Friends in Council." In it, mention is made of an old lady, who firmly believed that three pounds given by her were equal to about five pound ten given by anybody else. Her money had cost so much thought and so much rigid saving to get it together. Sixpence by sixpence had been got together through patient self-denial; each separate shilling had formed the matter of long consideration. And the old lady felt it hard that the result of all this should be hardly and unsympathetically expressed by such words as three pounds. Of course the philosophic reader knows that it was merely that the poor old lady felt an interest in what was her own, which she could not feel in what belonged to anybody else. Had she been a person of greater enlightenment, she would have read in all her own little anxieties and schemings, the reflection of what was passing in the minds of those around her; and she would have concluded not that three pounds of her own were equal to six pounds of a neighbor's; but rather that three pounds, no matter to whom belonging, made a serious and important thing. But the poor old lady's feeling was natural. I am not able, at the present moment, quite to repress a feeling entirely like it. It seems to me a far stranger thing that I should be here, than it would be that any one of a great many people I know should be here. They are venturesome folk. They go about a great deal. Nothing strikes them as very remarkable. When Mr. Smith said in my hearing, that something or other happened when he was going into Jerusalem, I could not but look at Mr. Smith with great respect. But Mr. Jones, who has been everywhere himself, was quite free from any such feeling. You would hear or read quite coolly, my friend, that A or B had been at the Land's End. It is no great matter. But come yourself to this very spot where I am sitting; look round on this scene on which I have cast my eyes since I wrote the last sentence; and if you be a homely person who have never been beyond the limits of Britain, and who lead a quiet life from day to day somewhere in a quiet rural parish in Scotland, you will feel it curious to find yourself here. And if you be a sensible person, you will not think it a fine thing to pretend that you do not feel it so.

You remember what Sydney Smith said of Scotland. He said, no doubt, many things on that subject; but the thing to which I refer is the statement that Scotland is "the knuckle-end of England." There is a certain degree of truth in the statement. After you have spent a little while in Surrey, or Sussex, or Wiltshire, in a very richly wooded part of either county; if you get into an express train on the North-Western Railway on the morning of a summer day, and travel on by daylight through Staffordshire and Lancashire, through Cumberland and Lanarkshire, till you arrive at Glasgow, you will be aware that Sydney Smith's metaphor corresponds with your own feeling. You will be aware that as you travel towards the North, the trees are gradually growing smaller, the fields less rich, the whole landscape barer and bleaker; you will remember that nightingales do not sing north of Leeds, and you will think of other little traces of something like a physical decadence. But the impression made upon you will vary according to the line of country you pass through. I could take you to tracts in Scotland where the trees and hedges and fields are as rich, and the air as soft and pleasant, as anywhere in Britain; and where you add to the charms of the sweet English landscape, the long summer twilights which England wants. The true knuckle-end of England is here. And you will feel *that*, if you come to this place through the rich plains traversed by the Great Western Railway; or (better still) by that railway which comes by Salisbury, Sherborne, and Honiton to Exeter, through a country where at every turn you feel you are looking on a landscape which is your very ideal of beautiful England; and where churches and churchyards abound, so incomparably lovely in architecture and situation, that on a pleasant summer day one could hardly wish for better than to sit down on an ancient tombstone, and look for an hour at the fair piece of gray Gothic, at the green ivy, and the great elms. And the churches come so frequently, that one cannot but think of the happy life of duty and leisure which may well be led by the unambitious country parson there. His population is probably so small that he is free from that constant sense of pressure under which the clergy in many places are now compelled to live. He may write his sermon without being worried by the thought of a dozen things waiting to be attended to; and he may sit down under a large tree in the churchyard and meditate, without knowing that meditation is a luxury in which he has not time to indulge. But come on towards the West, and you will find the gradual approach to the knuckle-end. The juiciness and richness of the leg of mutton, pass slowly into tendon, skin, and bone. In Devonshire, you have Scotch irregularity of outline in the landscape; but there is English luxuriance in the hedges and wild-flowers; and more than English softness in the air. You enter Cornwall, over Brunel's wonderful but remarkably ugly suspension bridge at Saltash; and you very soon feel that you have reached a tract entirely different from the ideal English country. The land is remarkably diversified in surface; steep ups and downs everywhere; and now and then, as you fly along in the railway train, you pass over a deep narrow gorge, spanned by the flimsiest wooden bridge that ever formed part of a line of railway. Sometimes these gorges are of vast depth. They occur perpetually; and they are always crossed by the like unsubstantial structures. For many miles after entering Cornwall, the country is very richly wooded. You may see all kinds of forest trees growing luxuriantly; and many orchards, thickly crowded with apple-trees. But after you have passed Truro, there is a total change. The engine pants and struggles, as it hardly draws the train up inclines of extraordinary steepness; and you begin to see all round you heather and granite; great bare stretches of country with tin mines here and there, and rare woods of stunted pine. The railway brings you to Penzance, a pretty little town ten miles from the Land's End, which has the advantage of a climate of wonderful mildness. Granite is the stone here; almost every building is formed of it. The town is situated at one side of a considerable bay. Across the bay, three miles off, is St. Michael's Mount, rising out of the sea. St. Michael's Mount, it will be remembered, was in former days the residence of the Giant Cormoran, whose destruction formed the first recorded exploit of Jack the Giant-Killer. You leave Penzance and journey westward; probably in a phaeton drawn by a black horse. There is a rich country for the first two or three miles; then you enter a district very bleak and desolate. The cottages are rude and squalid; the churches, all of granite, are rare and large; and look as if they were accustomed to be battered by heavy storms. You pass through the last village, which is about a mile from the sea; and then you go along a lane, through a great field whose surface is made of granite, heather, and yellow furze as short as heather. You see the sea before you, stretching far away; but the ground over which you are going swells so much, that it hides the rocky shore. Passing through that final large field, you might expect to come upon a sandy beach at last. At length you stand before a little cottage, an inscription on which tells you that it claims to be THE LAND'S END HOTEL: and here you will find the intelligent ostler, who guides you down a rough slope, not very steep, of granite, furze, and heather, till, after two hundred yards, you come upon the blunt promontory, whose extremity is by preëminence the End. The End does not reach into the sea so much as a hundred yards beyond the regular coast line. And the End is not the boldest portion of that rocky coast. Its height, as has been said, is about eighty feet perpendicular; while the rocks on either hand must be in many places at least a hundred and fifty. And now, looking back on the way you have come, you feel how gradually the scene around you grew barer, as you came on. It was like a bad man growing old. Trees and hedges were left behind; cornfields and cottages with little gardens; for the beautiful churches of Somersetshire, you have only that rude and stern erection which you passed a little since; and now you have come to this, that you have no more than granite, and furze, and desolate sea. It is a most interesting spot to come to visit for a little while; but it would be a terrible thing to be condemned to live here for the remainder of your life. I cannot but think here of the unloved and unhonored later days of some hoary reprobate; who, in a moral sense, has had his Somersetshire, then his Cornwall, and last his Land's End. And even though a man be not a reprobate, I believe that all life, apart from the presence of religion, is a going down hill. It is leaving behind, from year to year, the trees and flowers; leaving the soft green fields and the rich hedgerows; till you come at length to wastes of furze and heather; and end at last in stern rocks and pathless sea.

It was of this that the writer thought longest, sitting at the lonely Land's End; and this was something, let me confess, that never once occurred to me when reading Arnold's life, and musing on his theme for English verses. Another thing which will probably occur to the reader, when he shall visit the same place, will be, what a solitary and small being he himself will be there. The writer's home, at this moment, is seven hundred and forty miles away. Probably it is a good deal less, if you could go in a direct line; but such is the tale of the miles which he has traversed to reach the spot. And you will know, my friend, how misty and how far away your daily life and your home will seem, when you sit down by yourself in any lonely place, with all your belongings hundreds of miles distant. Going away alone, you truly leave great part of yourself behind. Your mere individuality is a very small thing in size. Great men, such as kings and nobles, have occasionally had this truth disagreeably impressed upon them. A man with a magnificent estate must feel as though those green glades and magnificent trees were a portion of himself, and as if you must see all these things, and add them to himself, before you can understand how big an object he really is. But small men feel that too. They feel as though, to reckon what they are, you must add to the little object that sense reveals to you, the path they have come through life; the labor they have come through; the griefs and joys they have felt; the atmosphere and the surroundings amid which they live at home. I thought of this, one afternoon last winter. The ground was covered with snow; it had grown almost dark; going down a steep street, in which were a good many passers-by, I beheld the dim form of a poor fellow who had but one arm. There he was, a little figure, walking along as fast as he could, going home. You would have said, a more thoroughly insignificant atom of humanity could hardly be. But I knew all about that man's humble home; and I knew how much depended on him there. Not many weeks before, his poor care-worn wife had died; and at that minute he was going home to his children, four little things, the eldest but seven years old, to whom he now had to be all. Anything befalling that insignificant man, would be to those four children an infinitely more important event than the separation of the Northern and Southern States of America. If we knew more about our humblest fellow-creatures, my reader; if we knew what they have borne and done, and what they have yet to bear and do; if round the unnoted little personality there were even the dim suggestion of its cares and belongings; we should feel more sympathy for every man; — we should regard no mortal as insignificant. I sometimes find people who talk of the great majority of their fellow-creatures as CADS; people who, in another country, would doubtless stand up vigorously for slavery. Let me say, that when I call to mind what I have known of those whom some heartless fools would call so; — when I think of their sufferings, their cares, their patience, their resignation, their sacrifices for one another; — my feeling towards the fools to whom I have alluded, passes from contempt, and turns to indignation. Would that we had all some of the truly Christian spirit of the heathen poet, who told us how much of sympathy with everything human he felt as incumbent upon him, forasmuch as he himself was a man!

But now, my friend, I must go. I shall never see the Land's End any more. But I have had it all to myself for these two hours; and it has become a possession forever. Yesterday it was a vague name; now, it is a clear picture, and it will always be so. It is not in the least like what I had expected. No person nor place you ever saw, is the least like what you expected. But now, I seem to have known it for a long time. And it is like parting from a friend to bid it good-by. But the black horse has rested, and has been fed; and I have far to go to-day.

Good-by!

CHAPTER IX.

CONCERNING RESIGNATION.

YOU know how a little child of three or four years old kicks and howls if it do not get its own way. You know how quietly a grown-up man takes it, when ordinary things fall out otherwise than he wished. A letter, a newspaper, a magazine, does not arrive by the post on the morning on which it had been particularly wished for, and counted on with certainty. The day proves rainy, when a fine day was specially desirable. The grown-up man is disappointed; but he soon gets reconciled to the existing state of facts. He did not much expect that things would turn out as he wished them. Yes; there is nothing like the habit of being disappointed, to make a man resigned when disappointment comes, and to enable him to take it quietly. And a habit of practical resignation grows upon most men, as they advance through life.

You have often seen a poor beggar, most probably an old man, with some lingering remains of respectability in his faded appearance, half ask an alms of a passer-by; and you have seen him, at a word of repulse, or even on finding no notice taken of his request, meekly turn away; too beaten and sick at heart for energy; drilled into a dreary resignation by the long custom of finding everything go against him in this world. You may have known a poor cripple, who sits all day by the side of the pavement of a certain street, with a little bundle of tracts in his hand, watching those who pass by, in the hope that they may give him something. I wonder, indeed, how the police suffer him to be there; for though ostensibly selling the tracts, he is really begging. Hundreds of times in the long day, he must see people approaching; and hope that they may spare him a half-penny; and find ninety-nine out of each hundred pass without noticing him. It must be a hard school of Resignation. Disappointments without number have subdued that poor creature into bearing one disappointment more with scarce an appreciable stir of heart. But on the other hand, kings, great nobles, and the like, have been known, even to the close of life, to violently curse and swear if things went against them; going the length of stamping and blaspheming even at rain and wind, and branches of trees and plashes of mud, which were of course guiltless of any design of giving offence to these eminent individuals. There was a great monarch, who when any little cross-accident befell him, was wont to fling himself upon the floor; and there to kick and scream and tear his hair. And around him, meanwhile, stood his awe-stricken attendants; all doubtless ready to assure him that there was something noble and graceful in his kicking and screaming, and that no human being had ever before with such dignity and magnanimity torn his hair. My friend Mr. Smith tells me that in his early youth he had a (very slight) acquaintance with a great Prince, of elevated rank and of vast estates. That great Prince came very early to his greatness; and no one had ever ventured, since he could remember, to tell him he had ever said or done wrong. Accordingly, the Prince had never learned to control himself; nor grown accustomed to bear quietly what he did not like. And when any one, in conversation, related to him something which he disapproved, he used to start from his chair, and rush up and down the apartment, furiously flapping his hands together, till he had thus blown off the steam produced by the irritation of his nervous system. That Prince was a good man; and so aware was he of his infirmity, that when in these fits of passion, he never suffered himself to say a single word; being aware that he might say what he would afterwards regret. And though he could not wholly restrain himself, the entire wrath he felt passed off in flapping. And after flapping for a few minutes, he sat down again, a reasonable man once more. All honor to him! For my friend Smith tells me that that Prince was surrounded by toadies, who were ready to praise everything he might do, even to his flapping. And in particular, there was one humble retainer, who, whenever his master flapped, was wont to hold up his hands in an ecstasy of admiration, exclaiming, "It is the flapping of a god, and not of a man!"

Now all this lack of Resignation on the part of princes and kings comes of the fact, that they are so far like children that they have not become accustomed to be resisted, and to be obliged to forego what they would like. Resignation comes by the habit of being disappointed, and of finding things go against you. It is, in the case of ordinary human beings, just what they expect. Of course, you remember the adage: "Blessed is he who expecteth nothing, for he shall not be disappointed." I have a good deal to say about that adage. Reasonableness of expectation is a great and good thing; despondency is a thing to be discouraged and put down as far as may be. But meanwhile let me say, that the corollary drawn from that dismal beatitude seems to me unfounded in fact. I should say just the contrary. I should say, "Blessed is he who expecteth nothing, for he will very likely be disappointed." You know, my reader, whether things do not generally happen the opposite way from that which you expected. Did you ever try to keep off an evil you dreaded, by interposing this buffer? Did you ever think you might perhaps prevent a trouble from coming, by constantly anticipating it; keeping, meanwhile an under-thought that things rarely happened as you anticipate them; and thus your anticipation of the thing might possibly keep it away? Of course you have; for you are a human being. And in all common cases, a watch might as well think to keep a skilful watchmaker in ignorance of the way in which its movements are produced, as a human being think to prevent another human being from knowing exactly how he will think and feel in given circumstances. We have watched the working of our own watches far too closely and long, my friends, to have the least difficulty in understanding the great principles upon which the watches of other men go. I cannot look inside your breast, my reader, and see the machinery that is working there; I mean the machinery of thought and feeling. But I know exactly how it works, nevertheless; for I have long watched a machinery precisely like it.

There are a great many people in this world who feel that things are all wrong, that they have missed stays in life, that they are beaten, — and yet who don't much mind. They are indurated by long use. They do not try to disguise from themselves the facts. There are some men who diligently try to disguise the facts, and who in some measure succeed in doing so. I have known a self-sufficient and disagreeable clergyman who had a church in a large city. Five sixths of the seats in the church were quite empty; yet the clergyman often talked of what a good congregation he had, with a confidence which would have deceived any one who had not seen it. I have known a church where it was agony to any one with an ear to listen to the noise produced when the people were singing; yet the clergyman often talked of what splendid music he had. I have known an entirely briefless barrister, whose friends gave out that the sole reason why he had no briefs was that he did not want any. I have known students who did not get the prizes for which they competed; but who declared that the reason of their failure was, that though they competed for the prizes, they did not wish to get them. I have known a fast young woman, after many engagements made and broken, marry as the last resort a brainless and penniless blackguard; yet all her family talk in big terms of what a delightful connection she was making. Now, where all that self-deception is genuine, let us be glad to see it; and let us not, like Mr. Snarling, take a spiteful pleasure in undeceiving those who are so happy to be deceived. In most cases, indeed, such trickery deceives nobody. But where it truly deceives those who practise it, even if it deceive nobody else, you see there is no true Resignation. A man who has made a mess of life has no need to be resigned, if he fancies he has succeeded splendidly. But I look with great interest, and often with deep respect, at the man or woman who feels that life has been a failure, — a failure, that is, as regards *this* world, — and yet who is quite resigned. Yes; whether it be the unsoured old maid, sweet-tempered, sympathetic in others' joys, God's kind angel in the house of sorrow, — or the unappreciated genius, quiet, subdued, pleased to meet even one who understands him amid a community which does not, — or the kind-hearted clever man to whom eminent success has come too late, when those were gone whom it would have made happy: I reverence and love, more than I can express, the beautiful natures I have known thus subdued and resigned!

Yes; human beings get indurated. When you come to know well the history of a great many people, you will find that it is wonderful what they have passed through. Most people have suffered a very great deal, since they came into this world. Yet, in their appearance, there is no particular trace of it all. You would not guess, from looking at them, how hard and how various their lot has been. I once knew a woman, rather more than middle-aged. I knew her well, and saw her almost every day, for several years, before I learned that the homely Scotchwoman had seen distant lands, and had passed through very strange ups and downs, before she settled into the quiet orderly life in which I knew her. Yet when spoken to kindly, by one who expressed surprise that all these trials had left so little trace, the inward feeling, commonly suppressed, burst bitterly out; and she exclaimed, "It's a wonder that I'm living at all!" And it is a wonder that a great many people are living, and looking so cheerful and so well as they do, when you think what fiery passion, what crushing sorrow, what terrible losses, what bitter disappointments, what hard and protracted work, they have gone through. Doubtless, great good comes of it. All wisdom, all experience, comes of suffering. I should not care much for the counsel of the man whose life had been one long sunshiny holiday. There is greater depth in the philosophy of Mr. Dickens, than a great portion of his readers discern. You are ready to smile at the singular way in which Captain Cuttle commended his friend Jack Bunsby as a man of extraordinary wisdom; whose advice on any point was of inestimable value. "Here's a man," said Captain Cuttle, "who has been more beaten about the head than any other living man!" I hail the words as the recognition of a great principle. To Mr. Bunsby, it befell in a literal sense; but we have all been (in a moral sense) a good deal beaten about the head and the heart before we grew good for much. Out of the travail of his nature; out of the sorrowful history of his past life; the poet or the moralist draws the deep thought and feeling which find so straight a way to the hearts of other men. Do you think Mr. Tennyson would ever have been the great poet he is, if he had not passed through that season of great grief which has left its noble record in "In Memoriam"? And a youthful preacher, of vivid imagination and keen feeling, little fettered by anything in the nature of good taste, may by strong statements and a fiery manner draw a mob of unthinking hearers; but thoughtful men and women will not find anything in all *that*, that awakens the response of their inner nature in its truest depths; they must have religious instruction into which real experience has been transfused; and the worth of the instruction will be in direct proportion to the amount of real experience which is embodied in it. And after all, it is better to be wise and good than to be gay and happy, if we must choose between the two things; and it is worth while to be severely beaten about the head, if *that* is the condition on which alone we can gain true wisdom. True wisdom is cheap at almost any price. But it does not follow at all that you will be happy (in the vulgar sense) in direct proportion as you are wise. I suppose most middle-aged people, when they receive the ordinary kind wish at New-Year's time of a Happy New Year, feel that *happy* is not quite the word; and feel *that*, too, though well aware that they have abundant reason for gratitude to a kind Providence. It is not *here* that we shall ever be happy; that is, completely and perfectly happy. Something will always be coming to worry and distress. And a hundred sad possibilities hang over us; some of them only too certainly and quickly drawing near. Yet people are content, in a kind of way. They have learned the great lesson of Resignation.

There are many worthy people who would be quite fevered and flurried by good fortune, if it were to come to any very great degree. It would injure their heart. As for bad fortune, they can stand it nicely, they have been accustomed to it so long. I have known a very hard-wrought man, who had passed, rather early in life, through very heavy and protracted trials. I have heard him say, that if any malicious enemy wished to kill him, the course would be to make sure that tidings of some signal piece of prosperity should arrive by post on each of six or seven successive days. It would quite unhinge and unsettle him, he said. His heart would go; his nervous system would break down. People to whom pieces of good luck come rare and small, have a great curiosity to know how a man feels when he is suddenly told that he has drawn one of the greatest prizes in the lottery of life. The kind of feeling, of course, will depend entirely on the kind of man. Yet very great prizes, in the way of dignity and duty, do for the most part fall to men who in some measure deserve them, or who at least are not conspicuously undeserving of them and unfit for them. So that it is almost impossible that the great news should elicit merely some unworthy explosion of gratified self-conceit. The feeling would in almost every case be deeper, and worthier. One would like to be sitting at breakfast with a truly good man, when the letter from the Prime Minister comes in, offering him the Archbishopric of Canterbury. One would like to see how he would take it. Quietly, I have no doubt. Long preparation has fitted the man who reaches that position for taking it quietly. A recent Chancellor publicly stated how *he* felt when offered the Great Seal. His first feeling, that good man said, was of gratification that he had fairly reached the highest reward of the profession to which he had given his life; but the feeling which speedily supplanted *that*, was an overwhelming sense of his responsibility and a grave doubt as to his qualifications. I have always believed, and sometimes said, that good fortune, not so great or so sudden as to injure one's nerves or heart, but kindly and equable, has a most wholesome effect upon human character. I believe that the happier a man is, the better and kinder he will be. The greater part of unamiability, ill-temper, impatience, bitterness, and uncharitableness, comes out of unhappiness. It is because a man is so miserable, that he is such a sour, suspicious, fractious, petted creature. I was amused, this morning, to read in the newspaper an account of a very small incident which befell the new Primate of England on his journey back to London after being enthroned at Canterbury. The reporter of that small incident takes occasion to record that the Archbishop had quite charmed his travelling companions in the railway carriage by the geniality and kindliness of his manner. I have no doubt he did. I am sure he is a truly good Christian man. But think of what a splendid training for producing geniality and kindliness he has been going through for a great number of years. Think of the moral influences which have been bearing on him for the last few weeks. We should all be kindly and genial, if we had the same chance of being so. But if Dr. Longley had a living of a hundred pounds a year, a fretful, ailing wife, a number of half-fed and half-educated little children, a dirty miserable house, a bleak country round, and a set of wrong-headed and insolent parishioners to keep straight, I venture to say he would have looked, and been, a very different man, in that railway carriage running up to London. Instead of the genial smiles that delighted his fellow-travellers (according to the newspaper story), his face would have been sour and his speech would have been snappish; he would have leaned back in the corner of a second-class carriage, sadly calculating the cost of his journey, and how part of it might be saved by going without any dinner. Oh, if I found a four-leaved shamrock, I would undertake to make a mighty deal of certain people I know! I would put an end to their weary schemings to make the ends meet. I would cut off all those wretched cares which jar miserably on the shaken nerves. I know the burst of thankfulness and joy that would come, if some dismal load, never to be cast off, were taken away. And I would take it off. I would clear up the horrible muddle. I would make them happy; and in doing *that*, I know that I should make them good!

But I have sought the four-leaved shamrock for a long time, and never have found it; and so I am growing subdued to the conviction that I never shall. Let us go back to the matter of Resignation, and think a little longer about *that*.

Resignation, in any human being, means that things are not as you would wish, and yet that you are content. Who has all that he wishes? There are many houses in this world in which Resignation is the best thing that can be felt any more. The bitter blow has fallen; the break has been made; the empty chair is left (perhaps a very little chair); and never more, while Time goes on, can things be as they were fondly wished and hoped. Resignation would need to be cultivated by human beings; for all round us there is a multitude of things very different from what we would wish. Not in your house, not in your family, not in your street, not in your parish, not in your country, and least of all in yourself, can you have things as you would wish. And you have your choice of two alternatives. You must either fret yourself into a nervous fever, or you must cultivate the habit of Resignation. And very often, Resignation does not mean that you are at all reconciled to a thing, but just that you feel you can do nothing to mend it. Some friend, to whom you are really attached, and whom you often see, vexes and worries you by some silly and disagreeable habit, — some habit which it is impossible you should ever like, or ever even overlook; yet you try to make up your mind to it, because it cannot be helped, and you would rather submit to it than lose your friend. You hate the East-wind; it withers and pinches you, in body and soul; yet you cannot live in a certain beautiful city without feeling the East-wind many days in the year. And that city's advantages and attractions are so many and great, that no sane man, with sound lungs, would abandon the city merely to escape the East-wind. Yet, though resigned to the East-wind, you are anything but reconciled to it.

Resignation is not always a good thing. Sometimes it is a very bad thing. You should never be resigned to things continuing wrong, when you may rise and set them right. I dare say, in the Romish Church, there were good men before Luther, who were keenly alive to the errors and evils that had crept into it, but who, in despair of making things better, tried sadly to fix their thoughts upon other subjects; who took to illuminating missals, or constructing systems of logic, or cultivating vegetables in the garden of the monastery, or improving the music in the chapel,—quietly resigned to evils they judged irremediable. Great reformers have not been resigned men. Luther was not resigned; Howard was not resigned; Fowell Buxton was not resigned; George Stephenson was not resigned. And there is hardly a nobler sight than that of a man who determines that he will NOT make up his mind to the continuance of some great evil; who determines that he will give his life to battling with that evil to the last; who determines that either that evil shall extinguish him, or he shall extinguish it! I reverence the strong, sanguine mind, that resolves to work a revolution to better things, and that is not afraid to hope it *can* work a revolution! And perhaps, my reader, we should both reverence it all the more that we find in ourselves very little like it. It is a curious thing, and a sad thing, to remark in how many people there is too much Resignation. It kills out energy. It is a weak, fretful, unhappy thing. People are reconciled, in a sad sort of way, to the fashion in which things go on. You have seen a poor, slaternly mother, in a way-side cottage, who has observed her little children playing in the road before it, in the way of passing carriages, angrily ordering the little things to come away from their dangerous and dirty play; yet when the children disobey her, and remain where they were, just saying no more, making no farther effort. You have known a master tell his man-servant to do something about stable or garden; yet when the servant does not do it, taking no notice: seeing that he has been disobeyed, yet wearily resigned, feeling that there is no use in always fighting. And I do not speak of the not unfrequent cases in which the master, after giving his orders, comes to discover that it is best they should not be carried out, and is very glad to see them disregarded; I mean when he is dissatisfied that what he has directed is not done, and wishes that it were done, and feels worried by the whole affair; yet is so devoid of energy as to rest in a fretful Resignation. Sometimes there is a sort of sense as if one had discharged his conscience by making a weak effort in the direction of doing a thing; an effort which had not the slightest chance of being successful. When I was a little boy, many years since, I used to think this; and I was led to thinking it by remarking a singular characteristic in the conduct of a school companion. In those days, if you were chasing some other boy who had injured or offended you, with the design of retaliation; if you found you could not catch him, by reason of his superior speed, you would have recourse to the following expedient. If your companion was within a little space of you, though a space you felt you could not make less, you would suddenly stick out one of your feet, which would hook round his, and he, stumbling over it, would fall. I trust I am not suggesting a mischievous and dangerous trick to any boy of the present generation. Indeed I have the firmest belief that existing boys know all we used to know, and possibly, more. All this is by way of rendering intelligible what I have to say of my old companion. He was not a good runner. And when another boy gave him a sudden flick with a knotted handkerchief, or the like, he had little chance of catching that other boy. Yet I have often seen him when chasing another, before finally abandoning the pursuit, stick out his foot in the regular way, though the boy he was chasing was yards beyond his reach. Often did the present writer meditate on that phenomenon, in the days of his boyhood. It appeared curious that it should afford some comfort to the evaded pursuer, to make an offer at upsetting the escaping youth,—an offer which could not possibly be successful. But very often, in after life, have I beheld, in the conduct of grown-up men and women, the moral likeness of that futile sticking out of the foot. I have beheld human beings who lived in houses always untidy and disorderly, or whose affairs were in a horrible confusion and entanglement, who now and then seemed roused to a feeling that this would not do; who querulously bemoaned their miserable lot, and made some faint and futile attempt to set things right; attempts which never had a chance to succeed, and which ended in nothing. Yet it seemed somehow to pacify the querulous heart. I have known a clergyman in a parish with a bad population, seem suddenly to waken up to a conviction that he must do something to mend matters, and set a-going some weak little machinery, which could produce no appreciable result, and which came to a stop in a few weeks. Yet that faint offer appeared to discharge the claims of conscience, and after it the clergyman remained a long time in a comatose state of unhealthy Resignation. But it is a miserable and a wrong kind of Resignation which dwells in that man, who sinks down, beaten and hopeless, in the presence of a recognized evil. Such a man may be in a sense resigned, but he cannot possibly be content.

If you should ever, when you have reached middle age, turn over the diary or the letters you wrote in the hopeful though foolish days when you were eighteen or twenty, you will be aware how quietly and gradually the lesson of Resignation has been taught you. You would have got into a terrible state of excitement, if any one had told you then that you would have to forego your most cherished hopes and wishes of that time, and it would have tried you even more severely to be assured that, in not many years you would not care a single straw for the things and the persons who were then uppermost in your mind and heart. What an entirely new set of friends and interests is that which now surrounds you, and how completely the old ones are gone! Gone, like the sunsets you remember in the summers of your childhood, — gone, like the primroses that grew in the woods where you wandered as a boy. Said my friend Smith to me a few days ago, "You remember Miss Jones and all about that? I met her yesterday, after ten years. She is a fat, middle-aged, ordinary-looking woman. What a terrific fool I was!" Smith spoke to me in the confidence of friendship, yet I think he was a little mortified at the heartiness with which I agreed with him on the subject of his former folly. He had got over it completely, and in seeing that he was (at a certain period) a fool, he had come to discern that of which his friends had always been aware. Of course early interests do not always die out. You remember Dr. Chalmers, and the ridiculous exhibition about the wretched little likeness of an early sweetheart, not seen for forty years, and long since in her grave. You remember the singular way in which he signified his remembrance of her, in his famous and honored age. I don't mean the crying, nor the walking up and down the garden-walk, calling her by fine names. I mean the taking out his card, — not his *carte*, you could understand *that;* but his visiting-card bearing his name, — and sticking it behind the portrait with two wafers. Probably it pleased him to do so, and assuredly it did harm to no one else. And we have all heard of the like things. Early affections are sometimes, doubtless, cherished in the memory of the old. But still, more material interests come in, and the old affection is crowded out of its old place in the heart. And so those comparatively fanciful disappointments sit lightly. The romance is gone. The midday sun beats down, and *there* lies the dusty way. When the cantankerous and unamiable mother of Christopher North stopped his marriage with a person at least as respectable as herself, on the ground that the person was not good enough, we are told that the future professor nearly went mad, and that he never quite got over it. But really, judging from his writings and his biography, he bore up under it, after a little, wonderfully well.

But looking back to the days which the old yellow letters bring back, you will think to yourself, Where are the hopes and anticipations of that time? You expected to be a great man, no doubt. Well, you know you are not. You are a small man, and never will be anything else, yet you are quite resigned. If there be an argument which stirs me to indignation at its futility, and to wonder that any mortal ever regarded it as of the slightest force, it is that which is set out in the famous soliloquy in *Cato*, as to the Immortality of the Soul. Will any sane man say, that if in this world you wish for a thing very much, and anticipate it very clearly and confidently, you are therefore sure to get it? If that were so, many a little schoolboy would end by driving his carriage and four, who ends by driving no carriage at all. I have heard of a man whose private papers were found after his death all written over with his signature as he expected it would be when he became Lord Chancellor. Let us say that his peerage was to be as Lord Smith. There it was, SMITH, C., SMITH, C., written in every conceivable fashion, so that the signature, when needed, might be easy and imposing. That man had very vividly anticipated the woolsack, the gold robe, and all the rest. It need hardly be said he attained none of these. The famous argument, you know, of course, is that man has a great longing to be immortal, and that therefore he is sure to be immortal. Rubbish! It is not true that any longing after immortality exists in the heart of a hundredth portion of the race. And if it were true, it would prove immortality no more than the manifold signature of SMITH, C., proved that Smith was indeed to be Chancellor. No; we cling to the doctrine of a Future Life,—we could not live without it; but we believe it, not because of undefined longings within ourselves, not because of reviving plants and flowers, not because of the chrysalis and the butterfly, but because "our Saviour, Jesus Christ, hath abolished death, and brought life and immortality to light through the gospel!"

There is something very curious and very touching, in thinking how clear and distinct, and how often recurring, were our early anticipations of things that were never to be. In this world, the fact is for the most part the opposite of what it should be to give force to Plato's (or Cato's) argument; the thing you vividly anticipate is the thing that is least likely to come. The thing you don't much care for, the thing you don't expect, is the likeliest. And even if the event prove what you anticipated, the circumstances and the feeling of it will be quite different from what you anticipated. A certain little girl three years old was told that in a little while she was to go with her parents to a certain city a hundred miles off, a city which may be called Altenburg as well as anything else. It was a great delight to her to anticipate that journey, and to anticipate it very circumstantially. It was a delight to her to sit down at evening on her father's knee, and to tell him all about how it would be in going to Altenburg. It was always the same thing. Always, first, how sandwiches would be made; how they would all get into the carriage (which would come round to the door), and drive away to a certain railway station; how they would get their tickets, and the train would come up, and they would all get into a carriage together, and lean back in corners, and eat the sandwiches, and look out of the windows, and so on. But when the journey was actually made, every single circumstance in the little girl's anticipations proved wrong. Of course, they were not intentionally made wrong. Her parents would have carried out to the letter, if they could, what the little thing had so clearly pictured and so often repeated. But it proved to be needful to go by an entirely different way and in an entirely different fashion. All those little details, dwelt on so much and with so much interest, were things never to be. It is even so with the anticipations of larger and older children. How distinctly, how fully, my friend, we have pictured out to our minds a mode of life, a home and the country round it, and the multitude of little things which make up the habitude of being, which we long since resigned ourselves to knowing could never prove realities! No doubt, it is all right and well. Even St. Paul, with all his gift of prophecy, was not allowed to foresee what was to happen to himself. You know how he wrote that he would do a certain thing, "as soon as I shall see how it will go with me!"

But our times are in the Best Hand. And the one thing about our lot, my reader, that we may think of with perfect contentment, is that they are so. I know nothing more admirable in spirit, and few things more charmingly expressed, than that little poem by Mrs. Waring which sets out that comfortable thought. You know it, of course. You should have it in your memory; and let it be one of the first things your children learn by heart. It may well come next after "O God of Bethel:" it breathes the self-same tone. And let me close these thoughts with one of its verses:

There are briers besetting every path,
  Which call for patient care:
There is a cross in every lot,
  And an earnest need for prayer:
But a lowly heart that leans on Thee,
  Is happy anywhere!

CHAPTER X.

CONCERNING THINGS WHICH CANNOT GO ON.

F course, in the full meaning of the words, Ben Nevis is one of the Things that cannot Go On. And among these, too, we may reckon the Pyramids. Likewise the unchanging ocean; and all the everlasting hills, which cannot be removed, but stand fast forever.

But it is not such things that I mean by the phrase; it is not such things that the phrase suggests to ordinary people. It is not things which are passing, indeed, but passing so very slowly, and with so little sign as yet of their coming end, that to human sense they are standing still. I mean things which even we can discern have not the element of continuance in them, — things which press it upon our attention as one of their most marked characteristics, that they have not the element of continuance in them. And you know there are such things. Things too good to last very long. Things too bad to be borne very long. Things which as you look at, you say to yourself, Ah, it is just a question of time! We shall not have *you* long!

This, as it appears to me, my reader, is the essential quality which makes us class anything among the Things which cannot Go On: it is that the thing should not merely be passing away, or even passing away fast; but that it shall bear on its very face, as the first thing that strikes us in looking at it, that it is so. There are passing things that have a sort of perennial look, — things that will soon be gone, but that somehow do not press it upon us that they are going. If you had met Christopher North, in his days of affluent physical health, swinging along with his fishing-rod towards the Tweed, you might, if you had reflected, have thought that in truth all *that* could not go on. The day would come when that noble and lovable man would be very different; when he would creep along slowly, instead of tearing along with that springy pace; when he would no longer be able to thrash pugnacious gypsies, nor to outleap flying tailors; when he would not sit down at morning in his dusty study, and rush through the writing of an article as he rushed through other things, impetuously, determinedly, and with marvellous speed, and hardly an intermission for rest; when mind and body, in brief, would be unstrung. But *that* was not what you thought of, in the sight of that prodigal strength and activity. At any rate, it was not the thought that came readiest. But when you see the deep color on the cheek of a consumptive girl, and the too bright eye; when you see a man awfully overworking himself; when you see a human being wrought up to a frantic enthusiasm in some cause, good or bad; when you find a lady declaring that a recently acquired servant, or a new-found friend, is absolute perfection; when you see a church, crowded to discomfort, passages and all, by people who come to listen to its popular preacher; when you go to hear the popular preacher for yourself, and are interested and carried away by a sermon, evincing such elaborate preparation as no man, with the duty of a parish resting upon him, could possibly find time for in any single week, — and delivered with overwhelming vehemence of voice and gesture; when you hear of a parish in which a new-come clergyman has set a-going an amount of parochial machinery which it would need at least three and probably six clergymen to keep working; when you see a family living a cat and dog life; when you see a poor fellow, crushed down by toil and anxiety, setting towards insanity; when you find a country gentleman, with fifteen hundred a year, spending five thousand; when you see a man submitting to an insufferable petty tyranny, and commanding himself by a great effort, repeated several times a day, so far as not just yet to let fly at the tyrant's head; when you hear of King Bomba gagging and murdering his subjects, amid the reprobation of civilized mankind; when you see the stoker of an American steamer sitting upon his safety-valve, and observe that the indicator shows a pressure of a hundred and fifty pounds on the square inch of his boiler, then, my friend, looking at such things as these, and beholding the end impending and the explosion imminent, you would say that these are Things which cannot Go On.

And then, besides the fact that in the case of very many of the Things which cannot Go On, you can discern the cause at work that must soon bring them to an end; there is a further matter to be considered. Human beings are great believers in what may be called the doctrine of Average. That is a deep conviction, latent in the ordinary mind, and the result of all its experience, that anything very extreme cannot last. If you are sitting on a winter evening in a chamber of a country house which looks to the north-east, and if a tremendous batter of wind and sleet suddenly dashes against the windows with a noise loud enough to attract the attention of everybody, I am almost sure that the first thing that will be said, by somebody or other, in the first momentary lull in which it is possible to hear, will be, "Well, *that* cannot last long." We have in our minds, as regards all things moral and physical, some idea of what is the average state of matters; and whenever we find any very striking deviation from *that*, we feel assured that the deviation will be but temporary. When you are travelling by railway, even through a new and striking country, the first few miles enable you to judge what you may expect. The country may be very different indeed from that which you are accustomed to see, day by day; but still, a little observation of it enables you to strike an average, so to speak, of that country. And if you come suddenly to anything especially remarkable, — to some enormously lofty viaduct, whence you look down upon the tops of tall trees and upon a foaming stream, or to some tunnel through a huge hill, or to some bridge of singular structure, or to some tract wonderfully wooded or wonderfully bare, — you involuntarily judge that all this is something exceptional, that it cannot last long, that you will soon be through it, and back to the ordinary jog-trot way.

And now, my friend, let me recall to mind certain facts connected with the great order of Things which cannot Go On; and let us compare our experience with regard to these.

Have you a residence in the country, small or great? Have you ever had such a residence? If you have one, or ever have had one, I have no doubt at all but there is or was a little gravelled walk, which you were accustomed often to walk up and down. You walked there, thinking of things painful and things pleasant. And if nature and training made you the human being for a country life, you found that that little gravelled path could do you a great deal of good. When you went forth, somewhat worried by certain of the little cares which worry at the time but are so speedily forgotten, and walked up and down, you found that at each turn you took, the path, with its evergreens at either hand, and with here and there a little bay of green grass running into the thick masses of green boughs and leaves, gently pressed itself upon your attention, — a patient friend, content to wait your time. And in a little space, no matter whether in winter or in summer, the path with its belongings filled your mind with pleasant little thoughts and cares, and smoothed your forehead and quieted your nervous system. I am a great believer in grass and evergreens and gravelled walks. Was it not pleasant, when a bitter wind was blowing outside your little realm, to walk in the shelter of the yews and hollies, where the air felt so snug and calm; and now and then to look out beyond your gate, and catch the bitter East on your face, and then turn back again to the warm, sheltered walk! Beautiful in frost, beautiful in snow, beautiful in rain, beautiful in sunshine, are clumps of evergreens, is green grass; and cheerful and healthful to our whole moral nature is the gravelled walk that winds between!

But all this is by the way. It is not of gravelled walks in general that I am to speak, but of one special phenomenon concerning such walks, and bearing upon my proper subject. If you are walking up and down a path, let us say a hundred and fifty yards long, talking to a friend, or holding conversation with yourself, — and if at each turn you take, you have to bend your head to pass under an overhanging bough, —

here is what will happen. To bend your head for once, will be no effort. You will do it instinctively, and never think about the matter. To stoop even six times, will not be much. But if you walk up and down for an hour, that constant evading of the overhanging bough will become intolerably irksome. For a little, it is nothing; but you cannot bear it, if it is a thing that is to go on. Here is a fact in human nature. You can stand a very disagreeable and painful thing for once; or for a little while. But a very small annoyance, going on unceasingly, grows insufferable. No annoyance can possibly be slighter than that a drop of cold water should fall upon your bare head. But you are aware that those ingenious persons, who have investigated the constitution of man with the design to discover the sensitive places where man can feel torture, have discovered what can be got out of that falling drop of water. Continue it for an hour; continue it for a day; and it turns to a refined agony. It is a thing which cannot go on long, without driving the sufferer mad. No one can say what the effect might be, of compelling a human being to spend a week, walking, through all his waking hours, in a path where he had to bend his head to escape a branch every minute or so. You, my reader, did not ascertain by experiment what would be the effect. However pretty the branch might be, beneath which you had to stoop, or round which you had to dodge, at every turn, that branch must go. And you cut away the blossoming apple-branch; you trained in another direction the spray of honeysuckle; you sawed off the green bough, beautiful with the soft beechen leaves. They had become things which you could not suffer to go on.

Have you ever been misled into living in your house, during any portion of the time in which it was being painted? If so, you remember how you had to walk up and down stairs on planks, very steep and slippery; how, at early morning, a sound pervaded the dwelling, caused by the rubbing your doors with stones, to the end of putting a smoother surface upon the doors; how your children had to abide in certain apartments underground, to be beyond the reach of paint and brushes and walls still wet. The discomfort was extreme. You could not have made up your mind to go on through life, under the like conditions; but you bore it patiently, because it was not to go on. It was as when you shut your eyes, and squeeze through a thicket of brambles, encouraged by the hope of reaching the farther side. So when you are obliged to ask a man to dinner, with whom you have not an idea or sympathy in common. Suppressing the tendency to yawn, you force yourself to talk about things in which you have not the faintest interest; and you know better than to say a word upon the subjects for which you really care. You could not stand this, were it not that from time to time you furtively glance at the clock, and think that the time of deliverance is drawing near. And on the occasion of a washing-day, or a change of cook, you put up without a murmur with a dinner to which you could not daily subdue your heart. We can go on for a little space, carried by the impetus previously got, and by the hope of what lies before us. It is like the dead points in the working of a steam-engine. You probably know that many river steamboats have but a single engine, and that there are two points, each reached every few seconds, at which a single engine has no power at all. The paddle-wheels continue to turn, in virtue of the strong impetus already given them. Now, it is plain to every mind, that if the engine remained for any considerable period at the point where it is absolutely powerless, the machinery driven by the engine would stop. But, in practice, the difficulty is very small, because it is but for a second or two that the engine remains in this state of paralysis. It does quite well for a little, but is a state that could not go on.

Any very extreme feeling, in a commonplace mind, is a thing not likely to go on long. Very extravagant likes and dislikes, very violent grief, such as people fancy must kill them, will, in most cases, endure not long. In short, anything that flies in the face of the laws which regulate the human mind, anything which is greatly opposed to Nature's love for the Average, cannot, in general, go on. I do not forget, that there are striking exceptions. There are people who never quite get over some great grief or disappointment; there are people who form a fixed resolution, and hold by it all through life. I have seen more than one or two men and women, whose whole soul and energy were so devoted to some good work, that a stranger, witnessing their doings for a few days and hearing their talk, would have said, "*That* cannot last. It must soon burn itself out, zeal like that!" But if you had made inquiry, you would have learned that all *that* had gone on unflagging, for ten, twenty, thirty years. There must have been sound and deep principle there at the first, to stand the wear of such a time; and you may well believe that the whole nature is now confirmed irretrievably in the old habit; you may well hope that the good Christian and philanthropist who has gone on for thirty years will go on as long as he lives, — will go on forever. But, as a general rule, I have no great faith in the stability of human character; and I have great faith in the law of Average. People will not go on very long, doing what is inconvenient for them to do. And I will back Time against most feelings and most resolutions in human hearts. It will beat them in the end. You are a clergyman, let us suppose. Your congregation are fond of your sermons. They have got into your way; and if so, they probably like to hear you preach better than anybody else; unless it be the two or three very great men. A family, specially attached to you, moves from a house near the church to another two or three miles away. They tell you, that nothing shall prevent their coming to their accustomed places every Sunday still: they would come, though the distance were twice as great. They are perfectly sincere. But your larger experience of such cases makes you well aware that time and distance and mud and rain and hot sunshine will beat them. Coming to church over that inconvenient distance, is a thing that cannot go on; it is a thing that ought not to go on; and you make up your mind to the fact. You cannot vanquish the laws of Nature. You may make water run up-hill, by laborious pumping. But you cannot go on pumping forever; and whenever the water is left to its own nature, it will certainly run down-hill. All such declarations as "I shall never forget you;" "I shall never cease to deplore your loss;" "I can never hold up my head again;" may be ethically true; but time will prove them logically false. The human being may be quite sincere in uttering them; but he will change his mind.

I do not mean to say that it is very pleasant to have to think thus; or that much good can come of dwelling too long upon the idea. It is a very chilling and sorrowful thing, to be reminded of all this in the hard, heartless way in which some old people like to drive the sad truth into the young. It is very fit and right that the girl of twenty, broken-hearted now because the young individual she is fond of is gone off to Australia, should believe that when he returns in five years he will find her unchanged, and should resent the remotest suggestion that by that time she will probably think and feel quite differently. It is fit and right that she should do all this, even though a prescient eye could discern that in two years exactly she will be married to somebody else, — and married, too, not to some old hunx of great wealth whom her parents have badgered her into marrying against her will, but (much worse for the man in Australia, who has meanwhile taken to drinking) married with all her heart to some fine young fellow, very suitable in age and all other respects. Yet, certain though the general principle may be, a wise and kind man or woman will not take much pleasure in imparting the sad lesson, taught by experience, to younger hearts. No good can come of doing so. Bide your time, my friend, and the laws of nature will prevail. Water will not long run up-hill. But while the stream is quite happy and quite resolute in flowing up an incline of one in twenty, there is no good in standing by it, and in roaring out that in a little while it will get tired of *that.* Experience tells us several things, which are not quite to the credit of our race; and it is wrong to chill a hopeful and warm heart with these. We should be delighted to find that young heart falsifying them by its own history: let it do so if it can.

And it is chilling and irritating to be often reminded of the refrigerating power of Time upon all warm feelings and resolutions. I have known a young clergyman, appointed early in life to his first parish, and entering upon his duty with tremendous zeal. I think a good man, however old, would rejoice at such a sight, would delightedly try to direct and counsel all that hearty energy, and to turn all that labor to the best account. And even if he thought within himself that possibly all this might not quite last, I don't think he would go and tell the young minister so. And the aged man would thankfully remember, that he has known instances in which all that *has* lasted; and would hope that in this instance it might last again. But I have known a cynical, heartless, time-hardened old man (the uncle, in fact, of my friend Mr. Snarling) listen with a grin of mingled contempt and malignity to the narration of the young parson's doings; and explain the whole phenomena by a general principle, inexpressibly galling and discouraging to the young parson. "Oh," says the cynical, heartless old individual, "new brooms sweep clean!" That was all. The whole thing was explained and settled. I should like to apply a new knout to the old individual, and see if it would cut smartly.

And then we are to remember, that though it be only a question of time with the existence of anything, *that* does not prove that the thing is of no value. A great part of all that we are enjoying consists of Things which cannot Go On. And though the wear that there is in a thing be a great consideration in reckoning its worth; and more especially, in the case of all Christian qualities, be the great test whether or not they are genuine; yet things that are going, and going very fast, have their worth. And it is very fit that we should enjoy them while they last, without unduly overclouding our enjoyment of them by the recollection of their evanescence. "Why," said an eminent divine, — "why should we pet and pamper these bodies of ours, which are soon to be reduced to a state of mucilaginous fusion?" There was a plausibility about the question; and for about half a minute it tended to make you think, that it might be proper to leave off taking your daily bath, and brushing your nails and teeth; likewise that instead of patronizing your tailor any further, it might be well to assume a horse-rug; and also that it might be unworthy to care for your dinner, and that for the future you should live on raw turnips. But of course, anything that revolts common sense, can never be a part of Christian doctrine or duty. And the natural reply to the rhetorical question I have quoted would of course be, that after these mortal frames are so fused, we shall wholly cease to care for them; but that meanwhile we shall suitably tend, feed, and clothe them, because it is comfortable to do so; because it is God's manifest intention that we should do so; because great moral and spiritual advantage comes of our doing so; and because you have no more right to disparage and neglect your wonderful mortal frame, than any other talent or gift confided to you by God.

Why should we neglect, or pretend to neglect, these bodies of ours, with which we are commanded to glorify God; which are bought with Christ's blood; which, even through the last lowliness of mortal dissolution, even when turned to dust again, are "still united to Christ;" and which are to rise again in glory and beauty, and be the redeemed soul's companion through eternity? And it is a mere sophism to put the shortness of a thing's continuance as a reason why it should not be cared for while it lasts. Of course, if it last but a short time, all the shorter will be the time through which we shall care for it. But let us make the best of things while they last; both as regards our care for them and our enjoyment of them.

That a thing will soon be done with, that the cloud will soon blow by, is a good reason for bearing patiently what is painful. But it is very needless to thrust in this consideration, to the end of spoiling the enjoyment of what is pleasant. I have seen people, when a little child, in a flutter of delighted anticipation, was going away to some little merrymaking, anxious to put down its unseemly happiness by severely impressing the fact, that in a very few hours all the pleasure would be over, and lessons would begin again. And I have seen, with considerable wrath, a cloud descend upon the little face at the unwelcome suggestion. What earthly good is to come of this piece of stupid, well-meant malignity? It originates, doubtless, in that great fundamental belief in many narrow minds, that the more uncomfortable you are the likelier you are to be right; and that God is angry when he sees people happy. Unquestionably, most of the little enjoyments of life are very transient. All pleasant social gatherings; all visits to cheerful country houses; all holidays; are things which cannot go on. No doubt, that is true; but that is no reason why we should sulkily refuse to enjoy them while they last. There is no good end secured, by persisting in seeing "towers decayed as soon as built." It is right, always latently, and sometimes expressly, to remember that they must decay; but meanwhile, let us be thankful for their shelter and their beauty. Sit down, happily, on a July day, beneath the green shade of your beeches; do not needlessly strain what little imagination you have, to picture those branches leafless, and the winter wind and clouds racking overhead. Enjoy your parcel of new books when it comes, coming not often; cut the leaves peacefully, and welcome in each volume a new companion; then carefully decide the fit place on your shelves where to dispose the pleasant accession to your store; and do not worry yourself by the reflection that when you die, the little library you collected may perhaps be scattered; and the old, friendly-looking volumes fall into no one knows whose hands; perhaps be set forth on out-door book-stalls; or be exhibited on the top of a wall, with a sack put over them when it begins to rain, as in a place which I have seen. "What is the use of washing my hands," said a little boy in my hearing; "they will very soon be dirty again!" Refuse, my reader, to accept the principle implied in the little boy's words, however specious it may seem. Whitewash your manse, if you be a Scotch minister, some time in April; paint your house in town, however speedily it may again grow black. Write your sermons diligently; write them on the very best paper you can get, and in a very distinct and careful hand; and pack them with attention in a due receptacle. It is, no doubt, only a question of time how long they will be needed, before the day of your departure shall make them no more than waste paper. Yet, though things which cannot go on, you may hope to get no small use out of them, to others and to yourself, before the time when the hand that travelled over the pages shall be cold with the last chill; and the voice that spoke these words shall be hushed forever. We know, obscurely, what we shall come to; and by God's grace we are content, and we hope to be prepared; but there is no need to overcast all life with the ceaseless anticipation of death. You may have read how John Hampden's grave was opened, at the earnest desire of an extremely fat nobleman who was his injudicious admirer. The poor wreck of humanity was there; and, as the sexton said, "We propped him up with a shovel at his back, and I cut off a lock of his hair." I hold with Abraham, who "buried his dead from his sight;" I hold with Shakspeare, who desired that no one should disturb him in his lowly bed, till He shall awaken him whose right it is to do so. Yet I read no lesson of the vanity of Hampden's life, in that last sad picture of helplessness and humiliation. He had come to *that;* yet all this does not show that his life was not a noble one while it lasted, though now it was done. He had his day; and he used it; whether well or ill let wiser men judge. And if it be right to say that he withstood tyranny, and helped to lay the foundation of his country's liberties, the whim of Lord Nugent and the propping up with the shovel can take nothing away from that.

You understand me, my friend. You know the kind of people who revenge themselves upon human beings who meanwhile seem happy, by suggesting the idea that it cannot last. You see Mr. A., delighted with his beautiful new church; you know how Miss B. thinks the man to whom she is to be married next week the handsomest, wisest, and best of mankind; you behold the elation of Mr. C. about that new pair of horses he has got; and if you be a malicious blockhead, you may greatly console yourself in the spectacle of the happiness of those individuals, by reflecting, and perhaps by saying, that it is all one of those things that cannot go on. Mr. A. will in a few months find no end of worry about that fine building; Miss B.'s husband, at present transfigured to her view, will settle into the very ordinary being he is; and Mr. C.'s horses will prove occasionally lame, and one of them a permanent roarer. Yet I think a wise man may say, I am aware I cannot go on very long; yet I shall do my best in my little time. I look at the right hand which holds my pen. The pen will last but for a short space; yet that is no reason why I should slight it now. The hand may go on longer. Yet, warm as it is now, and faithfully obeying my will as it has done, through all those years, the day is coming when it must cease from its long labors. And, for myself, I am well content that it should be so. Let us not strive against the silent current, that bears us all away and away. Let us not quarrel with the reminders we meet on many country gravestones, addressed unto us who are living from the fathers who have gone before. Yet you will think of Charles Lamb. He said (but nobody can say when Elia meant what he said), "I conceive disgust at those impertinent and unbecoming familiarities, inscribed upon your ordinary tombstones. Every dead man must take upon himself to be lecturing me with his odious truism, that 'Such as he now is I must shortly be.' Not so shortly, friend, perhaps, as thou imaginest. In the mean time I am alive. I move about. I am worth twenty of thee. Know thy betters!"

You may look on somewhat further, in a sweet country burying-place. Dear old church-yard, once so familiar, with the old oaks and the gliding river, and the purple hill looking over; where the true heart of Jeanie Deans has mouldered into dust; I wonder what you are looking like to-day! Many a time have I sat, in the quiet summer day, on a flat stone, and looked at the green graves; and thought that they were Things that could not Go On! *There* were the graves of my predecessors; the day would come when old people in the parish would talk, not unkindly, of the days, long ago, when some one was minister whose name is neither here nor there. But it was a much stranger thing to think, in that silent and solitary place, of the great stir and bustle there shall be in it some day! Here it has been for centuries; the green mossy stones and the little grassy undulations. But we know, from the best of all authority, that "the hour is coming" which shall make a total change. This quiet, this decay, this forgetfulness, are not to Go On!

We look round, my reader, on all our possessions, and all our friends, and we discern that there are the elements of change in all. "I am content to stand still," says Elia, "at the age to which I am arrived, — I and my friends; to be no younger, no richer, no handsomer. I do not want to be weaned by age, or drop like mellow fruit into the grave." There are indeed moods of mind in which all thoughtful men have possibly yielded to a like feeling; but I never heard but of one other man whose deliberate wish was just to go on in this round of life forever. Yet, though content to be in the wise and kind hands in which we are, we feel it strange to find how all things are going. Your little children, my friend, are growing older, — growing out of their pleasant and happy childhood; the old people round you are wrinkling up and breaking down. And in your constitution, in your way of life, there are things which cannot go on. There is some little physical malady, always rather increasing; and you cannot always be enlarging the doses of the medicine that is to correct it, or the opiates which make you sleep. I confess, with sorrow, that when I see an extraordinarily tidy garden, or a man dressed with special trimness, I cannot help looking forward to a day when all that is to cease; when the man will be somewhat slovenly, — when the garden will be somewhat weedy. I think especially of the garden; and the garden which comes most home to me is the manse garden. It was a marvel of exquisite neatness and order; but a new minister comes, who does not care for gardening, and all *that* goes. And though rejoicing greatly to see a parish diligently worked, yet sometimes I behold the parochial machinery driven with such a pressure of steam, that I cannot but think it never will last. I have known men who never could calmly think; who lived in a hurry and a fever. There are places where it costs a constant effort, not always a successful effort, to avoid coming to such a life; but let us strive against it. Let us not have constant push and excitement and high pressure. I hate to feel a whir around me, as of a huge cotton-mill. Let us "study to be quiet!"

And I have observed that clergymen who set that feverish machinery a-going, generally find it expedient to get away from it as speedily as may be, so as to avoid the discredit of its breaking down in their hands,—being well aware that it is a thing which cannot go on. We cannot always go on at a tearing gallop, with every nerve tense. Probably we are doing so a great deal too much. If so, let us definitively moderate our pace before the pace kills us.

"It's a long lane that has no turning," says the proverb, testifying to the depth of human belief in the Average, testifying to our latent conviction that anything very marked is not likely to go on. A great many people, very anxious and unhappy and disappointed, cherish some confused hope that surely all this has lasted so long, things must be going to mend. The night has been so long, that morning must be near, even though there be not the least appearance of the dawn as yet. If you have been a briefless barrister, or an unemployed physician, or an unbeneficed clergyman for a pretty long time, even though there be no apparent reason now, more than years since, why success should come, you are ready to think that surely it must be coming now, at last. It seems to be overdue, by the theory of Average. Yet it is by no means certain that there is a good time coming, because the bad time has lasted long. Still, it is sometimes so. I have known a man very laborious, very unfortunate, with whom everything failed; and after some years of this, I have seen a sudden turn of fortune come. And with exactly the same merit and the same industry as before, I have beheld him succeed in all he attempted, and gain no small eminence and reputation. "It behoved him to dree his weird," as was said by Meg Merrilies; and then the good time came. If you are happy, my reader, I wish your happiness may last. And if you are meanwhile somewhat down and depressed, let us hope that all this may prove one of the Things which cannot Go On!

"Shall I go on?" said Sterne, telling a touching story, familiar to most of us; and he answered his question by adding "No." "It is good" said an eminent author, "to make an end of a thing which might go on forever." And, on the whole, probably this Essay had better stop. And, at this genial season of kind wishes and old remembrances, we may fitly enough consider that these New Year's days cannot very often return to any. All this habitude of being cannot very long go on. Yet, in our little span here, we may gain possessions which never will fail. It is not a question of Time, with that which grows for Eternity! God grant each of us, always more assuredly, that Better Part which can Go On forever!

CHAPTER XI

CONCERNING CUTTING AND CARVING:

WITH SOME THOUGHTS ON TAMPERING WITH THE COIN OF THE REALM.

I BEHELD, as in a Vision, the following remarkable circumstances:

There was a large picture, by that great artist Mr. Q. R. Smith, hung up in a certain public place. It appeared to me that the locality partook of the nature of a market-place in a populous city: and numbers of human beings beheld the picture. A little vulgar boy passed, and looked at it: his words were these: "My eye! A'n't it spicy? Rather!" A blooming maiden gazed upon it, and her remark was as follows: "Sweetly pretty!" But a man who had long painted wagons for agricultural purposes, and who had recently painted a sign-board, after looking at the picture for a little, began to improve it with a large brush, heavily loaded with coarse red and blue, such as are used for painting wagons. Another man came, a house-painter: and he touched the picture, in several parts, with a brush filled with that white material which is employed for finishing the ceiling of rooms which are not very carefully finished. These persons, though horribly spoiling the picture, did honestly intend to improve it; and they fancied they had much improved it. Finally there came a malicious person, who was himself an artist; and who envied and hated the first artist for painting so well. As for this man, he busied himself upon the principal figure in the picture. He made its eyes horribly to squint. He put a great excrescence on its nose. He painted its hair a lively scarlet. And having hideously disfigured the picture, he wrote beneath it, *Q. R. Smith, pinxit.* And he pointed out the canvas to all his friends, saying, "That's Smith's picture: isn't it beautiful?"

Into this Vision I fell, sitting by the evening fire. The immediate occasion of this Vision was, that I had been reading a little volume, prettily printed and nicely bound, purporting to be "The Children's Garland from the Best Poets, selected and arranged by Coventry Patmore." There I had been pleasantly reviving my recollection of many of the pieces, which I had been taught to read and repeat as a boy at school. And as I read, a sense of wonder grew, gradually changing to a feeling of indignation. I said to myself, Surely Mr. Coventry Patmore's modesty has led him to take credit on his title-page for much less than he deserves. He has not merely selected and arranged these pieces from the Best Poets: he has also (according to his own ideas) *improved* them. We have (I thought), in this volume, the picture of Q. R. Smith, touched up with red and whitewash, and having the eyes and nose altered by the painter of signboards. Or, to speak more accurately, in reading this volume, we are requested to walk through a gallery of paintings by great masters, almost all improved, in many places, by the same painter of wagon-wheels, with the same large brush filled with coarse red. As we go on with the book, we come upon some poem which we have known all our lives, and every word of which is treasured and sacred in our memory. But we are made to feel that this is indeed our old friend: but his nose is cut off, and one of his eyes is put out. Such was my first hasty and unjust impression. Every poem of those I remembered from childhood had a host of verbal variations from the version in which I knew it. In Southey's well-known verses about "The Bell on the Inchcape Rock," I counted thirty-seven. There were a good many in Campbell's two poems; one called "The Parrot," and the other about Napoleon and the British sailor. So with Cowper's "Royal George:" so with Macaulay's "Armada." So with Scott's "Young Lochinvar:" so with Byron's "Destruction of Sennacherib:" so with Wordsworth's poem as to the dog that watched many weeks by his dead master on Helvellyn: so with Goldsmith's "Good people all, of every sort:" so with Mrs. Hemans' "Graves of a Household." Mr. Patmore tells us in his

Preface, that "in a very few instances he has ventured to substitute a word or phrase, where that of the author has made the piece in which it occurs unfit for children's reading." But, on my first reading of his book, it appeared that he had made alterations by scores, most of them so trivial as to be very irritating. But I proceeded to investigate. I compared Mr. Patmore's version of each poem with the version of each poem contained in the last edition of its author's works. And though I found a few variations, made apparently through careless transcribing: and though I was annoyed by considerable disregard of the author's punctuation and capitals; still it appeared that in the main Mr. Patmore gives us the pieces as their authors left them: while the versions of them, given in those books which are put into the hands of children, have, in almost every case, been touched up by nobody knows whom. So that when Mr. Patmore's book falls into the hands of men who made their first acquaintance with many of the pieces it contains in their schoolboy days, and who naturally prefer the version of them which is surrounded by the associations of that season: Mr. Patmore will be unjustly accused of having cut and carved upon the dear old words. Whereas, in truth, the present generation has reason to complain of having been introduced to the wrong things in youth: so that now we cannot rightly appreciate the right things. And for myself, my first unjust suspicion of

Mr. Patmore, speedily dispelled by investigation, led me to many thoughts upon the whole subject of literary honesty and dishonesty in this matter.

It seems to me quite essential that a plain principle of common faithfulness should be driven into those persons who edit and publish the writings of other men. If you pretend to show us Raphael's picture, let it be exactly as Raphael left it. But if your purpose be to exhibit the picture as touched up by yourself, do not mendaciously call the picture a Raphael. Call it what it is: to wit, Raphael altered and improved by Snooks. If you take a sovereign, and drill several holes in it, and fill them up with lead, you will be made to feel, should you endeavor to convey that coin into circulation, that though you may sell it for what it is worth as a sovereign plugged with lead, you had better not try to pass it off upon people as a genuine sovereign. All this is as plain as may be. But there are many collectors and editors of little poems, who take a golden piece by Goldsmith, Wordsworth, Campbell, or Moore: and punch out a word here and there, and stick in their own miserable little plug of pinchbeck. And then, having thus debased the coin, they have the impudence to palm it off upon the world with the superscription of Goldsmith, Wordsworth, Campbell, or Moore. It is needful, I think, that some plain principles of literary honesty should be instilled into cutting and carving editors. Even Mr. Palgrave, in his "Golden Treasury," is not free from some measure of blame; though his sins are as nothing compared with those of the editors of school collections and volumes of sacred poetry. Mr. Palgrave has not punched out gold to stick in pinchbeck: but in one or two glaring instances, he has punched out gold and left the vacant space. Every one knows that exquisite little poem of Hood's, "The Death Bed." That poem consists of four stanzas. Mr. Palgrave gives us in his book a poem which he calls "The Death Bed;" and puts at the end of it the honored name of Hood. But it is not Hood's "Death Bed:" any more than a sovereign with one half of it cut off would be a true sovereign. Mr. Palgrave gives us just two stanzas: Hood's first and last; leaving out the two intermediate ones. In a note, whose tone is much too confident for my taste, Mr. Palgrave attempts to justify this tampering with the coin of the realm. He says that the omitted stanzas are very ingenious, but that ingenuity is not in accordance with pathos. But what we want is Hood with his own peculiar characteristics: not Hood with the corners rubbed off to please even so competent a critic as Mr. Palgrave. In my judgment, the two omitted stanzas are eminently characteristic of Hood. I do not think they are very ingenious: they express simple and natural feelings: and they are expressed with a most touching and pathetic beauty. And on the whole, if you are to give the poem to the world as Hood's, they seem to have an especial right to stand in it. If you give a picture of a bison, surely you should give the hump: even though you may think the animal would be more graceful without it. We want to have the creature as God made it: with the peculiarities God gave it.

The poems which are cut and carved to the extremest degree are hymns. There is indeed some pretext of reason here: for it is necessary that hymns should be made, in respect of the doctrines they set forth, to fit the views of the people who are to sing them. Not that I think that this justifies the practice of adulterating the text. But in the few cases where a hymn has been altered so completely as to become virtually a new composition; and a much better composition than it was originally: and where the authorship is a matter really never thought of by the people who devoutly use the hymn; something is to be said for this tampering. For the hymn is not set forth as a poem written by this man or that: but merely as a piece which many hands may have brought into its present shape; and which in its present shape suits a specific purpose. You don't daub Raphael's picture with wagon paint; and still exhibit it as a Raphael. You touch it up according to your peculiar views: and then exhibit it saying merely, Is not that a nice picture? It is nobody's in particular. It is the joint doing of many men, and perhaps of many years. But where hymns are presented in a literary shape, and as the productions of the men who wrote them, the same law of honesty applies as in the case of all other literary work. I observe, with very great satisfaction, that in the admirable "Book of Praise" lately published by Sir Roundell Palmer, that eminent lawyer has made it his rule "to adhere strictly, in all cases in which it could be ascertained to the genuine uncorrupted text of the authors themselves." And Sir Roundell Palmer speaks with just severity of the censurable, but almost universal, practice of tampering with the text.

I confess that till I examined Mr. Patmore's volume, I had no idea to what an extent this literary clipping of the coin had gone, even in the matter of poetry for clipping and altering which there is no pretext of reason. It appears to me a duty, in the interest of truth, to protest against this discreditable cutting and carving. There are various editors of school-books, and other collections of poetry for the young, who seem incapable of giving the shortest poem by the greatest poet, without improving it here and there with their red brush. No statue is presented to us without first having its nose knocked off. And of course there is no necessity here for squaring the poems to some doctrinal standard. It is a pure matter of the editor's thinking that he can improve the compositions of Campbell, Wordsworth, Moore, Goldsmith, Southey, Scott, Byron, Macaulay, or Poe. So that in the case of every one of these manifold alterations the question is just this simple one: Whether

Wordsworth or some pushing Teacher of Elocution is the best judge of what Wordsworth should say: whether we are to hold by these great poets, believing that they most carefully considered their most careful pieces; or to hold by anybody who chooses to alter them. There is something intensely irritating in the idea of Mr. Smith, with his pencil in his hand, sitting down with a volume of Wordsworth, every word in every line of which was carefully considered by the great poet, and stands there because the great poet thought it the right word; and jauntily altering a word here and there. The vision still returns to me of the sign-painter touching up Raphael. But I have no doubt whatsoever that Mr. Smith or Mr. Brown thinks himself quite equal to improving Wordsworth. The self-sufficiency of human beings is wonderful. I have heard of a man who thought he could improve things better than anything of Wordsworth's. Probably you never heard of the youthful Scotch divine who lived in days when stupid bigotry forbade the use of the Lord's Prayer in the pulpits of the Scotch church. That young divine went to preach for an aged clergyman who was somewhat wiser than his generation: and who accordingly told the young divine in the vestry before service that the Lord's Prayer was habitually used in that church. "Is it necessary," said the young divine, "that I should use the Lord's Prayer?" "Not at all," replied the aged clergyman, "if you can use anything better." But the young divine was true to his party: and he used certain petitions of his own, which he esteemed as improvements on the Lord's Prayer.

You may be quite sure that in the compositions of any careful writer, you could not alter many words without injury to the writer's style. You could make few alterations which the writer would approve. In a careful style, rely on it, there was some appreciable reason present to the author's mind for the employment of almost every word; and for each word's coming in just where it does. This is true even of prose. And I should fancy that few men would long continue to write for any periodical the editor of which was wont to cut and carve upon their articles. You remember how bitterly Southey used to complain of the way in which Lockhart altered his. But all this holds good with infinitely greater force in the case of poetry: especially in the case of such short gems as many of those in Mr. Patmore's volume. The prose writer, however accurate, covers his pages a day: each sentence is carefully weighed; but weighed rapidly. But the poet has lingered long over every word in his happiest verse. How carefully each phrase has been considered: how each phrase is fitted to all the rest! I declare it seems to me, there is something sacred in the best stanzas of a great poet. It is profanation to alter a word. And you know how to the sensitively strung mind and ear of the author a single wrong note makes discord of the whole: the alteration of a word here and there may turn the sublime to the ridiculous. And such alterations may be made in all good faith, by people whose discernment is not sharpened to this particular use. There was a pretty song, popular some years ago, which was called "What are the wild waves saying?" The writer had many times heard that song: but he hardly recognized its name when he heard it once asked for by the title of "What are the mad waves roaring?" Let us have the poet's work as he left it. You do not know how painfully the least verbal alteration may jar upon a sensitive ear. I hold that so sacred is the genuine text of a great poet, that even to the punctuation; and the capital letters, however eccentric their use may be; it should be esteemed as sacrilege to touch it. Let me say here that no man who does not know the effect upon poetry of little typographical features is fit to edit any poet. It seems to me that Mr. Coventry Patmore fails there. It is plain that he does not perceive, with the sensitiveness proper to the editor of another man's poetry, what an effect upon the *expression* of a stanza or a line is produced by typographical details. Mr. Patmore not unfrequently alters the punctuation which the authors (we may suppose) adopted after consideration; and which has grown, to every true reader of poetry, as much a part of the stanza as its words are. Every one knows how much importance Wordsworth attached to the use of capital letters. Now, in the poem entitled "Fidelity" ("Children's

Garland,") Mr. Patmore has at *nine* different places substituted a small letter for Wordsworth's capital: considerably to the destruction of the expression of the piece: and at any rate to the clipping of the coin Wordsworth left us. In the last verse of Poe's grand poem, "The Raven," Mr. Patmore has, in six lines, made *five* alterations: one quite uncalled for; *four* for the worse. Poe wrote *demon:* Mr. Patmore chooses to make it *dæmon.* Poe wrote "the shadow that *lies* floating on the floor:" Mr. Patmore substitutes *is* for *lies:* to the detriment of the sense. And Poe ends the stanza thus:

And my soul from out that shadow that lies floating on the floor
Shall be lifted — nevermore!

It is extraordinary how many variations for the worse Mr. Patmore introduces into the last line. He makes it

Shall be lifted "Nevermore."

1st. The dash before the *nevermore* is omitted: a loss.

2d. The *Nevermore* is made to begin with a capital: which, though very right in preceding stanzas, is here absurd.

3d. The *Nevermore* is marked as a quotation: which it is not. It is one in the preceding stanzas, and is properly marked as one: but here the mark of quotation is wrong.

4th. Poe puts, most fitly, a mark of exclamation

after the *nevermore!* If ever there was a stanza which should end with that point, it is here. But Mr. Patmore, for no earthly reason, leaves it out.

Now, some folk may say these are small matters. I beg to say that they are *not* small matters to any accurate reader: and above all, to any reader with an eye for the *expression* of poetry. And no man, who has not an eye for these minute points, and who does not feel their force, is fit for an editor of poetry. I am quite sure that no mortal, with an eye for such niceties, will deny, that each of Mr. Patmore's *four* alterations of one line of Poe is an alteration for the worse. I have taken as the proper representation of Poe the best American edition of his whole works, in four volumes. But if you look at the beautiful little edition of his poems, edited by Mr. Hannay, you will find that the accurate scholar has given that stanza exactly as the American edition gives it: and, of course, exactly right. If Mr. Patmore does not understand how indescribably irritating these little cuttings and carvings are to a careful reader or writer, he is not the man to edit the "Children's Garland," or any other collection of poetry. Every one can imagine the indignation with which Wordsworth the scrupulous and Poe the minutely accurate would have learned that their best poems were, either through carelessness, or with the design of making them better, altered by Mr. Patmore, even in the matter of capital letters and points: and that finally the result was to be exhibited to the world, not as Raphael touched up by Smith the sign-painter, but as Raphael pure and genuine.

And while thus fault-finding at any rate, I am obliged to say that though acquitting Mr. Patmore of any vainglorious purpose of improving those "Best Poets" from whom he has selected his "Garland," I cannot acquit him of culpable carelessness in a good many instances. Though he may not have smeared the great master's picture with red paint, he has not been sufficiently careful to present the picture to us unsmeared by anybody else. Except in those "very few instances" in which he has changed a word or phrase "unfit for children's reading," we have a right to expect an accurate version of the text. But it is quite easy to point out instances in which Mr. Patmore's reading could not have been derived from any edition of the poet, however bad; nor can any one say that Mr. Patmore's reading is an improvement upon the *textus receptus*. The third and fourth lines of Macaulay's poem, "The Armada," run as follows:

> When that great fleet invincible against her bore in vain
> The richest spoils of Mexico, the stoutest hearts of Spain.

Mr. Patmore makes two alterations in these lines. For *that great fleet*, he reads *the great fleet*, to the detriment alike of rhythm and meaning. And for *the richest spoils of Mexico*, he reads *the richest stores*. It is extremely plain that *spoils* is a much better word than *stores*. It was not the *stores* of Mexico; that is, the wealth stored up in Mexico; that the Armada bore. It was the *spoils* of Mexico; that is, the wealth which the Spaniards had taken away from Mexico; that the Armada bore. It is possible that the Spaniards may have taken away *all* the wealth of Mexico: in which case the *spoils* and the *stores* would coincide in fact. But they would still be totally different in conception; and so exact a writer as Macaulay would never confound the two things.

Next, let us turn to Campbell's touching verses entitled "The Parrot." Campbell put at the top of his verses the words, "The Parrot: a domestic Anecdote." Mr. Patmore puts the words, "The Parrot: a true Story." The poem tells us, very simply and beautifully, how a certain parrot, which in its early days had been accustomed to hear the Spanish language spoken, was brought to the island of Mull: where, we may well suppose, it heard no Spanish. It lived in Mull for many years, till its green and gold changed to gray: till it grew blind and apparently dumb. But let the story be told in the poet's words:

> At last, when blind and seeming dumb,
>   He scolded, laugh'd, and spoke no more,
> A Spanish stranger chanced to come
>   To Mulla's shore;
> He hail'd the bird in Spanish speech,
>   The bird in Spanish speech replied,
> Flapp'd round his cage with joyous screech,
>   Dropt down, and died.

In glancing over Mr. Patmore's reading of this little piece, I am annoyed by observing several alterations in Campbell's punctuation: every alteration manifestly for the worse. But there is a more serious tampering with the text. The moral of the poem, of course, is that parrots have hearts and memories as well as we. And the poem sets out by stating that great principle. The first verse is:

> The deep affections of the breast,
> That Heaven to living things imparts,
> Are not exclusively possess'd
> By human hearts.

Mr. Patmore has the bad taste, not to say more, to leave that verse out. I cannot see any good reason why. The principle it states is one which a word or two would render quite intelligible to any child. Indeed, to any child who could not take in that principle, the entire story would be quite unintelligible. And I cannot recognize Mr. Patmore's treatment of this poem as other than an unjustifiable tampering with the coin of the realm.

There is another poem of Campbell's which fares as badly. Campbell calls it "Napoleon and the British Sailor." Mr. Patmore, in his zeal for cutting and carving, calls it "Napoleon and the Sailor: a true Story." This poem, like the last, sets out with a principle or sentiment; and then goes on with the facts. Mr. Patmore takes it upon himself to leave out that first verse: and then to daub the second verse in order to make it intelligible in the absence of the first. I hold this to be utterly unpardonable. It is emphatically Raphael improved by the sign-painter. And the pretext of anything "unfit for children's reading" will not hold here. Any child that coul1 understand the story, would understand this first verse·

I love contemplating — apart
From all his homicidal glory,
The traits that soften to our heart
Napoleon's story!

Then Campbell's second verse runs thus:

'Twas while his banners at Boulogne
Armed in our island every freeman,
His navy chanced to capture one
Poor British seaman.

Thus simply and naturally does the story which follows, rise out of the sentiment which the poet has expressed. But as Mr. Patmore has cut out the sentiment, he finds it necessary to tamper with the second verse: and accordingly he starts in this abrupt, awkward, and ugly fashion; which no true reader of Campbell will behold without much indignation: and which would have roused the sensitive poet himself to still greater wrath: —

Napoleon's banners at Boulogne
Armed in our island every freeman,
His navy chanced,

And so on. Here, you see, in the verse as improved by Mr. Patmore, we have two distinct propositions; separated by a comma. Mr. Patmore not merely has no eye for punctuation; but is plainly ignorant of its first principles. If any schoolboy, after having had the use of the colon and semicolon explained to him, were to use a comma in such fashion in an English theme, he would richly deserve a black mark for stupidity; and he would doubtless receive one. But apart from this lesser matter, which will not seem small to any one with a sense of grammatical accuracy, I ask whether it be not too bad that Campbell's natural and beautiful verse should be adulterated into this irritating caricature of it.

Let us next test Mr. Patmore's accuracy in exhibiting Sir Walter Scott. Everybody knows "Lady Heron's Song" which Sir Walter himself called "Lochinvar:" but which Mr. Patmore, eager for change, calls "Young Lochinvar." Sir Walter's first two lines are these:

> O, young Lochinvar is come out of the west,
> Through all the wide Border his steed was the best.

Mr. Patmore cannot render these simple lines accurately. He begins *West* with a capital letter: which, right or wrong, Sir Walter did not. Then he puts a point of exclamation after *West*, where Sir Walter has a comma. Sir Walter tells us that Lochinvar's *steed was the best:* Mr. Patmore improves the statement into *his steed is the best.* The very pettiness of these changes makes them the more irritating. Granting that Mr. Patmore's reading is neither better nor worse than the original, why not leave us the poem as the great man gave it us? Through all that well-known song, one is worried by Mr. Patmore's wretched little smears of red paint. The punctuation throughout is no longer matter for an imposition: it is matter for a flogging. Sir Walter says,

So *boldly* he entered the Netherby Hall:

Mr. Patmore with his brush makes it *so bravely.* And, eager for change at any price, Mr. Patmore gives us a new spelling of the name of the river Esk. Sir Walter, like everybody else, spells that word *Esk.* Mr. Patmore is not content with this, but develops the word into *Eske.* Sir Walter describes a certain locality as *Cannobie Lee:* Mr. Patmore improves the name into *Cannobie* LEA. And finally, the song ending with a question, Sir Walter ends it with a point of interrogation. But Mr. Patmore, impatient of the restraints of grammar, concludes with a point of exclamation.

All this is really too bad. Byron fares no better: and Mr. Patmore's alterations are of the same irritating and contemptible kind. Byron wrote

And there lay the steed with his nostril all wide,
But through it there roll'd not the breath of his pride;

Mr. Patmore cannot leave this alone. In the first line he reads *nostrils* for *nostril:* in the second, *them* for *it.* Now, not only are Byron's words the best, just because Byron chose them: but Byron's description is strikingly true to fact. Every one who has ever seen a horse fallen, or a horse dead, knows how remarkably *flat* the creature lies upon the ground. It is startling to find the sixteen hands of height when the animal was upon his legs, turned to something that hardly surpasses your knee when the creature is lying upon his side. And the head of a dead horse, lying upon the ground, would show *one* nostril and not *two.* You would see only the upper one : and remark that the warm breath of the creature was no longer rolling through *that.* These little matters make just the difference between being accurate and being inaccurate: between being right and being wrong.

I do not know whether it be from a desire to improve Mr. Keble's name, that Mr. Patmore, in his "Index of Writers," alters it to *Keeble.* I object likewise to Mr. Patmore's improving Barnfield's couplet

> She, poor bird, as all forlorn,
> Leaned her breast up till a thorn:

by substituting *against* for *up till.* The very stupidest child would know, after one telling, the meaning of *up till:* and Mr. Patmore's alteration is a destruction of the antique flavor of the piece.

The thoughtful reader, who has had some experience of life, must have arrived at this conviction: that if two or three slices of a leg of mutton are extremely bad, all the rest of the leg is probably bad too. I have not examined the whole of Mr. Patmore's volume: but I am obliged to conclude, from the absence of minute accuracy in the pieces which I have examined, that the entire volume is deficient in minute accuracy. Now, in a book like this, accuracy is the first thing. If any scholar were to take up a play of Æschylus or Aristophanes, and find it as carelessly edited as several of the poems which we have considered, I think the scholar would be disposed to throw that play into the fire. And I cannot for my life see why perfect accuracy should be less sought after by an editor of English poems than by an editor of Greek plays.

But on the general question of cutting and carving I would almost go so far as to say, that after a poem has been current for years, and has found a place in many memories, not even its author has a right to alter it. Nothing, at least, but an improvement the most extraordinary, can justify such a breaking in upon a host of old associations. It is a mortifying thing, when a man looks, in later life, into the volume of his favorite author, to find that the things he best remembers are no longer there. Even manifest improvement cannot reconcile us to the change. When the present writer was a youth at College, he cherished an enthusiastic admiration for John Foster's "Essays." Let it be said, his admiration is hardly less now. I read and re-read them in a large octavo volume: one of the earlier editions, which had not received the author's latest corrections. Yet I valued every phrase:

and I well remember how aggrieved I felt when I got an edition with Foster's final emendations; and found that Foster had cut out, and toned down, and varied, just the things of which my memory kept the firmest hold. One feels as though one had a vested interest in what had been so prized and lingered over. You know how Wordsworth and Moore kept touching up their verses: generally for the worse. I do not think the last edition which Wordsworth himself corrected, is the best edition of his poetry. In that poem of his which has already been named, concerning the faithful dog on Helvellyn, he made, late in life, various little changes: which not being decidedly for the better, must be held as for the worse. For any change from the dear old way is for the worse, unless it be very markedly for the better. And surely, after describing the finding of the poor tourist's body, the old way, which was this:

> Sad sight! the shepherd, with a sigh,
> Looks round, to learn the history:

is quite as good as the new way, which is this:

> The appalled Discoverer with a sigh,
> Looks round, to learn the history.

No rule, indeed, can be laid down here. No great poet cuts and carves upon his own productions so much as Mr. Tennyson. You remember how

> Revered Victoria, you that hold —

has changed into

Revered, beloved, oh you that hold.

You remember how in the story of the schoolboys who stole a litter of pigs, the passage,

We paid in person, scored upon that part
Which cherubs want.

has now dropped all reference to the scoring. And "Locksley Hall" bristles with verbal alterations, which every careful reader of Tennyson knows. One bows, of course, to the presence of Mr. Tennyson; and does not venture to set up one's own taste as against his. Yet, let me confess it, I miss and I regret some of the old things. Doubtless there are passages which at the first were open to hostile criticism, and which met it: which now have been raised above all cavil. There is that passage in the "Dream of Fair Women," which describes the death of Iphigenia. She tells of it herself. Here is the verse as it stands even in the seventh edition:

The tall masts quivered as they lay afloat,
The temples and the people and the shore;
One drew a sharp knife thro' my tender throat
Slowly, — and nothing more.

Every one feels how unpleasant is the picture conveyed by the last two lines. It passes the limits of tragedy, and approaches the physically revolting It

.s, likewise, suggestive rather of the killing of a sheep or pig, than of the solemn sacrifice of a human being. I confess, I incomparably prefer the simplicity of the inspired statement: "And Abraham stretched forth his hand, and took the knife to slay his son." We don't want any details as to how the knife was to be used; or as to the precise point at which it was to let out life. It would jar, were we to read, "Abraham stretched forth his hand, and was just going to cut Isaac's throat." Now Mr. Tennyson is worse than that: for he gives us, doubtless with painful accuracy, the account of the actual cutting of the throat. Then, besides this, Mr. Tennyson's verse, as it used to stand, was susceptible of a wrong interpretation. I do not mean that any candid reader would be likely to mistake the poet's sense: but I mean that an ill-set critic would have occasion for misrepresenting it. You may remember that a severe critic *did* misrepresent it. In an ancient Review, you may see the verse printed as I have given it above: and then the critic goes on to say something like this: "What an unreasonable person Iphigenia must have been! 'He cut my throat: nothing more:' what more could the woman possibly want?" Of course, *we* know what the poet meant: but, in strictness, what he meant he did not say. But look to the latest edition of Mr. Tennyson's poems; and you will be content. Here is the verse now. You will see that it has been most severely cut and carved; but to a most admirable result:

The high masts trembled as they lay afloat;
  The towers, the temples wavered, and the shore;
The bright death quivered at the victim's throat,
  Touched, and I knew no more.

I should fancy, my friend, that you have nothing to say against such tampering with the coin. This is as though a piece of baser metal were touched with the philosopher's stone, and turned to gold. And there have been cases in which a very felicitous change has been made by one man upon the writing of another. A single touch has sometimes done it. I wonder whether Mr. Palgrave was aware that, in giving in his book those well-known verses "To Althea from Prison," which he rather absurdly describes as by *Colonel* Lovelace (why does he not tell us that his extracts from a greater poet are by William Shakspeare, *Esquire?*), there is one verse which he has not given as Lovelace wrote it,

When I lie tangled in her hair
  And fetter'd to her eye,
The birds, that wanton in the air,
  Know no such liberty.

Lovelace wrote "the *gods* that wanton in the air:" and *birds* was substituted by Bishop Percy. It is a simple and obvious substitution: and the change is so greatly and so unquestionably for the better, that it may well be accepted: as indeed it has universally been.

The mention of a happy substitution naturally suggests the most unhappy substitution on record. You may remember how the great scholar, Bentley, puffed up by his success in making emendations on Horace and Terence, unluckily took it upon himself to edit Milton. And here indeed, we have, with a vengeance, Raphael improved by the painter of wagons. Milton wrote, as everybody knows :

> No light, but rather darkness visible:

but Bentley, eager to improve the line, turns it to

> No light, but rather *a transpicuous gloom.*

There is another passage in which the contrast between the master and the wagon-painter is hardly less marked. Where Milton wrote,

> Our torments also may in length of time
> Become our elements:

Bentley, as an improvement, substituted the following remarkable passage,

> Then, *as 'twas well observed,* our torments may,
> Become our elements.

It is to be admitted that the stupidity of Bentley's reading, is even surpassed by its impudence. Of course, the principle taken for granted at the beginning of such a work is, that Bentley's taste and judgment were better than Milton's. For, you observe, there was no pretext here of restoring a more accurate reading, lost through time: there was no pretext of giving more exactly what Milton wrote. There was no question as to Milton's precise words: but Bentley thought to make them better. And there is something insufferable in the picture of the self-satisfied old Don, sitting down in his easy-chair with "Paradise Lost:" and, pencil in hand, proceeding to improve it. Doubtless he was a very great classical scholar: but unless his wits had mainly forsaken him when he set himself to edit Milton, it is very plain that he never could have been more than an acute verbal critic. Thinking of Bentley's "Milton," one imagines the Apollo Belvedere put in a hair-dresser's window, with a magnificent wig: and dressed in a suit of clothes of the very latest fashion. I think likewise of an incident in the life of Mr. N. P. Willis, the American author. When he was at college in his youth, the head of his college kept a white horse, which he was accustomed to drive in a vehicle of some kind or other. Mr. N. P. Willis and his companions surreptitiously obtained temporary possession of the horse; and painted it crimson, with a blue mane and tail. I confess that I like Mr. N. P. Willis better for that deed, than for anything else I ever heard of his doing: and I may mention, for the satisfaction of my younger readers, that the colors used in painting the horse were of such a nature, that they adhered to the animal for a lengthened period, notwithstanding all endeavors to remove them. Now Dr. Bentley, in editing Milton, did as it were paint the white horse crimson and blue; and then exhibited it to the world, saying, "That is Smith's fine horse!" Nor should it be accepted as any apology for like conduct on the part of any editor, that the editor in good faith has such a liking for these colors, that he thinks a horse looks best when it looks blue and crimson. And though the change made by an editor be not of such a comprehensive nature as the painting of an entire horse anew, but rather consists of a multitude of little touches here and there;—as points changed, capitals left out, and *whiches* for *thats;* still the result is very irritating. You know that a very small infusion of a foreign substance can vitiate a thing. Two drops of prussic acid in a cup of water: two smears of red paint across the Raphael: affect the whole. I know hardly any offence, short of great crime, which seems to me deserving of so severe punishment, as this of clipping the coin of the realm of literature.

There is something, too, which irritates one, in the self-sufficient attitude which is naturally assumed by a man who is cutting and carving the composition of another. It is an evil which attends all reviewing, and which a modest and conscientious reviewer must feel keenly, that in reviewing another man's book, you seem to assume a certain superiority to him. For in every case in which you find fault with him, you are aware that the question comes just to *this,*—whether your opinion or his is worth most. To which may be added the further question: whether you or he have devoted most time and thought to forming a just opinion on this particular point. But when a man sits down not merely to point out an author's faults, but to correct them; the assumption of superiority is more marked still. And everybody knows that the writings of great geniuses have been unsparingly cut and carved by very inferior men. You know how Byron sent "The Siege of Corinth" to Mr. Gifford, giving him full power to alter it to any extent he pleased. And you know how Mr. Gifford did alter it; by cutting out all the good passages and leaving all the bad. The present writer has seen a man in the very act of cutting and carving. Once upon a time I entered a steamer which was wont to ply upon the waters of a certain noble river, that winds between Highland hills. And entering that bark, I beheld a certain friend, seated on the quarter-deck, with a little volume in his hand. I never saw a man look more entirely satisfied with himself than did my friend; as he turned over the leaves of the little volume in a hasty, skipping fashion; and jauntily scribbled here and there with a pencil. I beheld him in silence for a time, and then asked what on earth he was doing. "Oh," said he, "I am a member of the committee appointed by the Great Council to prepare a new book of hymns to be sung throughout the churches of this country. And this little volume is a proof copy of the hymns suggested: and a copy of it is sent to each member of the committee to receive his emendations. And as you see, I am beguiling my time in sailing down the river by improving these hymns." In this easy manner did my friend scribble whatever alterations might casually suggest themselves, upon the best compositions of the best hymn writers. Slowly and laboriously had the authors written those hymns, carefully weighing each word; and weighing each word perhaps for a very long time. But in the pauses of conversation, with no serious thought whatsoever, but willing to testify how much better he knew what a hymn should be than the best authors of that kind of literature, did my friend set down his random thoughts. Give me that volume, said I, with no small indignation. He gave it to me, and I proceeded to examine his improvements. And I can honestly say that not merely was every alteration for the worse; but that many of the alterations testified my friend's utter ignorance of the very first principles of metrical composition; and that all of them testified the extreme narrowness of his acquaintance with that species of literature. Some of the verses, as altered by him, were astounding specimens of rhythm. The only thing I ever saw which equalled them was a stanza by a local poet, very zealous for the observance of the Lord's day. Here is the stanza:

Ye that keep horses, read psalm 50;
To win money on the Sabbath day, see that ye never be so thrifty!

In Scotland we have a psalter and a hymnal imposed by ecclesiastical authority: so that in all parish churches there is entire uniformity in the words of praise. But it worries one to enter a church in England, and to find, as one finds so often, that the incumbent has published a hymnal, the sale of which he insures by using it in his church; and all the hymns in which are cut and carved to suit his peculiar doctrinal and æsthetical views. The execrable taste and the remarkable ignorance evinced in some of these compilations, have on myself, I confess, the very reverse of a devotional effect. And the inexpressible badness of certain of the hymns I have seen in such volumes, leads me to the belief that they must be the original compositions of the editor himself. There is an excellent little volume of Psalms and Hymns, collected by Mr. Henry Herbert Wyatt, of Trinity Chapel, Brighton; but even in it, one is annoyed by occasional needless changes. In Bishop Heber's beautiful hymn, which begins "From Greenland's icy mountains," Mr. Wyatt has smeared the third verse. The Bishop wrote, as every one knows,

> Shall we, whose souls are lighted
>   With wisdom from on high,—
> Shall we to men benighted
>   The lamp of life deny?

But Mr. Wyatt substitutes *can* for the *shall* with which the first and third lines begin: a change which no man of sense can call an improvement. A hymn to which I always turn, as one that tests an editor, is Bishop Ken's incomparable one, commonly called the "Evening Hymn." I find, with pleasure, that Mr. Wyatt has not tried to improve it: save that he has adopted an alteration which has been all but universally accepted. Bishop Ken wrote,

All praise to Thee, my God this night:

while most of us, from childhood, have been taught to substitute *Glory* for *All Praise*. And this is certainly an improvement. Glory, *gloria*, is certainly the right word with which to begin an ascription of praise to the Almighty. If not in itself the fittest word, the most ancient and revered associations of the Christian Church give it a prescriptive right to preference. A hymn which no man seems able to keep his sacrilegious hands off is Charles Wesley's hymn,

Jesu, lover of my soul.

I observe Mr. Wyatt makes three alterations in the first three lines of it, — each alteration for the worse. But I begin to be aware that no human being can be trusted to sit down with a hymn-book and a pencil, with leave to cut and carve. There is a fascination about the work of tampering: and a man comes to change for what is bad rather than not change at all. There are analogous cases. When I dwelt in the country, I was once cutting a little path through a dense thicket of evergreens; and a friend from the city, who was staying with us, went out with me to superintend the proceedings. Weakly, I put into my friend's hands a large and sharp weapon, called in Scotland a *scutching-knife:* and told him he might smooth off certain twigs which projected unduly on the path. My friend speedily felt the fascination of cutting and carving. And after having done considerable damage, he restored me the weapon, saying he felt its possession was a temptation too strong for him to resist. When walking about with the keen sharp steel in his hand, it was really impossible to help snipping off any projecting branch which obtruded itself upon the attention. And the writer's servant (dead, poor fellow: one of the worthiest though most unbending of men) declared, with much solemnity and considerable indignation, that in forming a walk he would never again suffer the scutching-knife to be in any other hands than his own. Now, it is a like temptation that assails the editor of hymns: and even if the editor is a competent man (and in most cases he is not) I don't think it safe to trust him with the scutching-knife. The only editor of hymns whom the writer esteems as a perfect editor, is Sir Roundell Palmer. For Sir Roundell starts with the determination to give us each hymn exactly as its author left it. It is delightful to read "All praise to Thee, my God, this night:" and to come upon

Jesu, lover of my soul,
Let me to Thy bosom fly:

after "Jesu, *Saviour* of my soul:" and "Jesus *refuge* of my soul." I remark, in Sir Roundell's book, occasional signs of having taken a hymn from an early edition of the author's works: which, in later editions was retouched by the author himself. Thus James Montgomery's "Friend after friend departs," is given as first published: not as the author left it. In the four verses, Montgomery made *five* alterations: which are not shown in Sir Roundell's work. But, as one who feels much interest in hymnal literature, and who has given some attention to it, I cannot refrain from saying that in the matter of faithfulness, Sir Roundell Palmer's book is beyond question or comparison the best. There is nothing second, third, or tenth to it. It is first; and the rest are nowhere.

Having mentioned the best hymnal that I know, one naturally thinks of the worst. There is a little volume purporting to be *Hymns collected by the Committee of the General Assembly on Psalmody:* published at Edinburgh in 1860. It is to be remembered that the Church of Scotland has never approved this little volume: the committee have published it on their own responsibility. Mr. Wyatt, in making his collection, tells us he examined thirty thousand hymns, and took the best of them. Sir Roundell Palmer also gives us in his volume the best hymns in the language. But neither Mr. Wyatt nor Sir Roundell (both most competent judges) have seen fit to admit much of the matter contained in this little compilation. So we may conclude, either that Mr. Wyatt did not find some of these compositions among his thirty thousand: or that, having examined them, he did not think them worthy of admission to his collection of about two hundred and fifty hymns. Sir Roundell Palmer's hymns number four hundred and twelve: and he has not erred on the side of exclusion: yet he has excluded a good many of the Scotch eighty-five. Out of the first fifteen of the Scotch book, fourteen are unknown to him. And I do not think cutting and carving ever went to a length so reprehensible, as in this volume. As to the fitness of the hymns for use in church, opinions may possibly differ: but I am obliged to say that I never saw any collection of such pieces so filled with passages in execrable taste, and utterly unfit for Christian worship.

It may amuse my readers, to show them George Herbert improved. Everybody knows the famous poem, "The Elixir." It consists of six verses. The Scotch reading consists of four. In the first verse, three verbal alterations, intended as improvements, are made on Herbert. "Teach me, my God and king," becomes, "Teach *us*, *our* God and king." The second verse in the Scotch reading, is unknown to Herbert. It is the doing of some member of the committee. The gold has been punched out, and a piece of pinchbeck has been put in. Herbert's third verse is omitted. Then comes the well-known verse:

> All may of Thee partake:
> Nothing can be so mean,
> Which, with this tincture, FOR THY SAKE,
> Will not grow bright and clean.

This is improved as follows:

> All may of Thee partake;
>   Nothing *so small can be,*
> *But draws, when* ACTED *for Thy sake,*
>   *Greatness and worth from Thee.*

You will doubtless think that Herbert pure is better than Herbert improved by the sign-painter. But the next verse is smeared even worse. Who does not remember the saintly man's words:

> A servant with this clause,
>   Makes drudgery divine:
> Who sweeps a room, as for Thy laws,
>   Makes that, and the action, fine.

But, as Sam Weller remarked of Mr. Pickwick in a certain contingency, "his most formiliar friend voodnt know him," as thus disguised:

> If done beneath Thy laws,
>   Even humblest labors shine:
> Hallowed is toil, if this the cause,
>   The meanest work, divine.

Herbert's temper, we know, was angelic: but I wonder what he would have looked like, had he seen himself thus docked, and painted crimson and blue. No doubt, "The Elixir," as the master left it, is not fitted for congregational singing. But that is a reason for leaving it alone: it is no reason for thus unpardonably tampering with the coin of the realm.

There are various pieces in this unfortunate work, whose appearance in it I can explain only on this theory. Probably, some day when the committee met, a member of committee produced a manuscript, and said that here was a hymn of his own composition; and begged that it might be put in the book. The other members read it, and saw it was rubbish: but their kindly feeling prevented their saying so: and in it went. One of the last things many people learn, is not to take offence when a friend declines to admire their literary doings. I have not the faintest idea who are the members of the committee which issued this compilation. Likely enough, there are in it some acquaintances of my own. But that fact shall not prevent my saying what I honestly believe: that it is the very worst hymn-book I ever saw. I cannot believe that the persons who produced it, could ever have paid any attention to hymnal literature: they have so thoroughly missed the tone of all good hymns. Indeed, many of the hymns seem to be formed on the model of what may be called the Scotch "Preaching Prayer:" the most offensive form of devotion known; and one entirely abandoned by all the more cultivated of the Scotch clergy. I heard, indeed, lately, an individual pray at a meeting about the Lord's day. In his prayer, he alluded to the Lancashire distress: and informed the Almighty that the patience with which the Lancashire people bore it was very much the result of their being trained in Sunday-schools. But, leaving this volume, which is really not worth farther notice, let me mention, that in the first twelve lines of

"Jesu, lover of my soul," there are *ten* improvements made on Wesley. "While the tempest still is high," has *nigh* substituted for *high*. "Till the storm of life is past," is made "Till the *storms* of life *are* past." "Oh receive my soul at last," has *And* substituted for *Oh:* for no conceivable reason. And the familiar line, "Hangs my helpless soul on Thee," has been turned, by the wagon-painter, into "*Clings* my helpless soul *to* Thee." I ask any intelligent reader, Is not this too bad? All my readers know that I am a clergyman of the Church of Scotland, for whose use these hymns have been so debased and tampered with. They never shall be sung in my church, you may rely on it. And the fact, that this cutting and carving has been done so near home, serves only to make me the more strongly to protest against it.

If it were not far too large a subject to take up now, I should say something in reprobation of the fashion in which many people venture to cut and carve upon words far more sacred than those of any poet: I mean upon the words of Holy Scripture. Many people improve a scriptural text or phrase when they quote it: the improvement generally consisting in giving it a slight twist in the direction of their own peculiar theological views. I have heard of a man who quoted as from Scripture the following words: "It is appointed unto all men once to die; and after death *Hell*." It was pointed out to him that no such statement exists in Scripture: the words which follow the mention of death being, "and after this the judgment." But the misquoter of Scripture declined to accept the correction, declaring that he thought his own reading was better. I have heard of a revival preacher who gave out as his text the words "Ye shall all likewise perish." Every one will know what a wicked distortion he made of our Saviour's warning in thus clipping it. And I have heard texts of Scripture pieced together in a way that made them convey a meaning just as far from that of the inspired writers, as that conveyed by the well-known mosaic, "And Judas departed, and went and hanged himself:" "Go thou and do likewise."

Probably the reader is tired of the subject. I thank him for his patience in following me so far: and I shall keep him no longer from something more interesting.

CONCLUSION.

I WAS sitting by my study fire this evening in a rocking-chair, in the restful interval between dinner and tea, and thinking how I should conclude this volume. In that meditative state, my attention was drawn to a little girl who was sitting on the floor a little way off, sewing, and at the same time talking to herself.

These were her words ; — they were spoken slowly, in a pensive tone, and with considerable pauses between the sentences.

"Once I thought a great deal of a shilling. Now, I think nothing of it. I am accustomed to shillings. I think nothing even of a pound. I have got one myself, and I thing nothing of it."

You see, the freshness and edge of enjoyment were gone, through habit. Shillings had become too many, and so they were not now the great things they used to be. And after all, it was no very great number of shillings which had sufficed to produce this result.

Listening to the little girl's meditation, I thought of

my volume. It is still a curious feeling to see one's thoughts in print. The page that bears what you have yourself written, my friend, has always a peculiar expression, — an expression that is familiar and yet strange. And there is still more of the singular feeling it imparts, when you look at an entire volume of your own. But more than one or two have preceded this, and the writer begins to feel towards a volume as the little girl said she felt towards a shilling. Yet not quite as the little girl said she felt. The freshness is somewhat gone, yet the publication of a new book is a little epoch in a quiet life. I suppose the Editor of a daily newspaper, seeing himself in print every day of his life, if he pleases, and often finding it his duty to write upon subjects in which he feels no great personal interest, must cease, in a few years, to feel any special attraction to the columns that have come from his own pen. There is less likelihood of *that*, in the case of a writer whose productions see the light at much longer intervals. And you may remember how Southey, who wrote probably more in quantity than any English author of the present century, with but two or three exceptions, tells us that he retained to the last the keen interest of a quite fresh writer in his own articles. When a new *Quarterly* appeared, he was quite impatient if it were a day too late in reaching him. I have no doubt he cut all the leaves before reading any, for Southey was a man of an orderly turn; but

I am sure he read his own paper the first. And he says he always found it very fresh and interesting reading, and he conveys that he generally thought it very good. As indeed it was. The shillings did not lose their value, many as they might grow.

There have been cases in which the successive shillings grew always more precious. You will think of Sterne, who appreciated his own writings so highly, and who used to write to his friends, as he was drawing each succeeding volume of "Tristram Shandy" to a close, that this new volume was to be by far the best. The present writer can say sincerely that each succeeding volume of these Essays, which you may have read, has been the result of more care and thought. He does not write now in the vague hope that perhaps somebody may read what he writes; he has the certainty of finding very many kindly readers. And he is not able to write now in the unconstrained way in which he wrote the first of those chapters, in days when not one of his rustic parishioners ever saw a page which he put forth. He is conscious now of the check which comes of the pervading sense, that a great many of the flock intrusted to his care recognize in what he writes a familiar hand, and can compare what is written on these pages with what it is his duty to teach them elsewhere. He ventures to believe that, in spirit, there is no inconsistency. And he knows that in the judgment of those whose judgment he values most, there is none.

There is but little time, in the life of a hard-working parish clergyman, for writing anything beyond that which it is imperative to write. And one may sometimes think, with a wearied sigh, even in the midst of duty which is very dear, of the learned quiet and leisure of canonries and deaneries, such as our poor Church has not, — sadly despoiled of that which is by right her own. Yet the habit of the pen grows into a second nature, and reserved folk never talk out their heart so freely as when talking to all the world. And if we live, friendly reader, I think we shall meet again.

THE END.

www.ingramcontent.com/pod-product-compliance
Lightning Source LLC
LaVergne TN
LVHW020225110826
845151LV00003B/834

* 9 7 8 1 4 2 5 5 3 2 0 4 8 *